C000295547

REDUCE OR STOP DRINKING WITH MEDICATION: THE HOW-TO GUIDE

Book 3

From the

RETHINKING DRINKING

Book Series

LINDA BURLISON

ADDICTION PUBLISHING

FIRST EDITION, VERSION 3.01

Copyright © 2016 by Linda Burlison/Addiction Publishing

ISBN 978-0-9971076-4-7 Electronic Book Text
ISBN 978-0-9971076-5-4 Paperback

Reduce or Stop Drinking with Medication: The How-To Guide / by Linda Burlison. – 1st Edition

Addiction Publishing, New York, N.Y.

Ordering
Special discounts are available on quantity purchases. For details, contact the publisher. Orders by trade bookstores and wholesalers welcome.

Publisher
Addiction Publishing
http://www.AddictionPublishing.com
linda@aprescriptionforalcoholism.com

Book Website
http://www.APrescriptionForAlcoholics.com

Reproduction & Permissions
No part of this book may be reproduced or transmitted in any form or by any means, electronic or mechanical, including photocopying, recording or by any information storage and retrieval system, without written permission from the author, except in the case of brief quotations embodied in critical reviews and certain other noncommercial uses permitted by copyright law. For permission requests, contact the publisher.

WHAT THE EXPERTS SAID

"It is highly disturbing that this drug is not made available to the patients that need it."[1]

–Report in Pharmacology & Therapeutics, 2006

•••

"There is an enormous gap between the number of alcohol use disorder patients [alcoholics] who would potentially benefit from medications and the number of patients who actually receive medications ... a recent study ... showed that nationally, only 3% of Veterans Health Administration patients with alcohol use disorder received treatment medications."[2]

–Report in American Journal of Psychiatry, 2014

•••

"There is no other comparable example in medicine where you *have* evidence-based treatments that are *not available*."[3]

–Dr. Shelly Greenfield, MD, Chief Academic Officer, McLean Hospital; Professor of Psychiatry, Harvard Medical School, 2012

•••

"People with addictive disorders continue to be offered, with great certitude and frequently at great cost, 'treatments' that are unsubstantiated by data or already known to be without beneficial effects...Meanwhile, advances that may be modest but have solid scientific support are arrogantly rejected by treatment providers in ways that would cause an uproar in other areas of medicine."[4]

–Dr. Markus Heilig, M.D., Ph.D., Former Chief of the Laboratory of Clinical Studies, and a Clinical Director at the US Institute of Alcohol Abuse, 2015

·····

"No experimental studies unequivocally demonstrated the effectiveness of AA or [12-step] approaches for reducing alcohol dependence… People considering attending AA or TSF [Twelve Step] programs should be made aware that there is a lack of experimental evidence on the effectiveness of such programs."[5]

–2006 Cochrane Review (Cochrane is one of the most credible and trusted scientific/medical review organizations in the world)

·····

"I'm not trying to eliminate AA…I'm just saying it should be prescribed to that tiny group who can make use of it… It's terribly harmful when you send 90 percent of the people for the wrong treatment advice."[6]

–Toronto Star article quoting Dr. Lance Dodes, Retired Professor of Psychiatry, Harvard Medical School, 2014

·····

"Medication-assisted treatment has shown much promise in reducing alcohol use and promoting abstinence in patients diagnosed with alcohol use disorder. Considerable research evidence and consensus among experts support the use of pharmacologic treatments…

A number of FDA-approved medications have been shown to be important elements of such treatment.

Although some patients do not benefit from medication-assisted treatment, most do. For each patient deemed an appropriate candidate for medication-assisted treatment, multiple pharmacologic agents offer a variety of options so that treatment can be tailored to each patient's needs and circumstances."[7]

–Free Guide from the Center for Substance Abuse Treatment, Substance Abuse and Mental Health Services Administration, US Department of Health and Human Services, 2013

IMPORTANT LEGAL NOTICES

Affiliations & Endorsements

The publisher and author are not affiliated with, do not endorse, nor recommend any products, brands, brand names, medications, substances, trademarks, companies, individuals, institutions, journals, doctors, writers, scientists, authors, personnel, or any industry (collectively, 'Third Parties') mentioned herein.

Third Parties mentioned herein belong to their respective owners, and are used without permission. Their use and any reference to, comment on, or mention of a Third Party is not intended to imply any endorsement of or direct (or indirect) affiliation with the Third Party.

Views expressed are solely the author's own. No Third Party has authorized, sponsored, or endorsed the content herein.

Risk

The reader ('you') expressly acknowledge and agree that neither the author nor the publisher nor its corporation ('we') are responsible for the results of your decisions resulting from the use of the Book, '*A Prescription for Alcoholics–Medications for Alcoholism*' ('the Book') or associated materials including forums or associated websites ('Related Materials'). Collectively, the Book and Related Materials shall be referred to as 'the content'.

Your use of the content acknowledges acceptance of these restrictions, disclaimers, and limitations. Use of the content is at your own risk.

We make no claim as to the accuracy of this information. You acknowledge that we have no control of or responsibility for your use of the content; have no knowledge of the specific or unique circumstances under which the content may be used by you; undertake no obligation to supplement or update the content of the book or related materials.

You assume all risk for selection and use of the content provided and for ensuring the appropriateness of using and relying upon the information in view of attendant circumstances, indications, and contraindications.

No Representation or Warranty

Except for warranties which may not be disclaimed as a matter of law, we make no representation or warranties whatsoever, express or implied, including but not limited to: representations or warranties regarding the accuracy or nature of the content; warranties of title; noninfringement; merchantability or fitness for a particular purpose; completeness; accuracy; reliability; completeness, suitability or availability with respect to the content of this book. We do not warrant that the information is true, current or non-misleading.

Every effort has been made to ensure that all information is accurate and complete, but no guarantee is made to that effect. We shall not be responsible for any errors, misstatements, inaccuracies or omissions regarding content. The content does not endorse any drug, pharmacy, diagnose patients, or recommend treatment.

References are provided for informational purposes only and do not constitute an endorsement of any websites or other sources. The websites listed may change. We are not medical or healthcare professionals.

Not a Substitute for Medical Advice

Methods described are the author's personal thoughts and are nothing more than an expression of information found in published research and the opinions of the author. They are not intended to be construed as medical or health advice and should not be treated as such. Information is observation-only and has not been supported by scientific studies or clinical trials unless otherwise stated. It is intended to help readers be better informed consumers of health care and to provide general medical information for informational purposes only. You must not rely on the information as an alternative to medical advice from a doctor or healthcare provider or use it to diagnose or treat any medical condition.

If you have questions of a medical nature, you should consult your doctor in all instances. If you are suffering from a medical condition, seek immediate professional medical attention. Do not delay seeking medical attention, or disregard professional medical advice or discontinue medical treatment because of information in this book. Do not stop or start medications, or change dosage without first consulting a physician since doing so could be hazardous to your health. For diagnosis or treatment of any medical problem, consult your own physician.

This content is not intended to be a substitute for the medical advice of a licensed physician. Healthcare practitioners should use professional judgment in using the information provided. You must not rely on the information to choose to seek or not to seek professional medical care; or to choose or not choose specific treatment. The absence of a warning for a given drug or combination thereof in no way should be construed to indicate that the drug or combination is safe, effective or appropriate for you. Drug information contained herein may be time sensitive. Different individuals respond to medication in different ways.

Under no circumstances are we responsible for, nor liable (to any person including but not limited to the end-user and persons treated by or on behalf of the end-user) for: any specific health needs that may require medical supervision; any direct, indirect, exemplary, special or consequential loss or damages or negative consequences (collectively, "Losses") of any nature from any treatment, action, application or preparation, to any person relating to the end-user's use of the information in this book. The end-user agrees to indemnify and hold us harmless from any claims, lawsuits, proceedings, costs, attorney's fees, arising out of or relating to the end-user's use of the information in this book in all cases including but not limited to losses for tort, personal injury, medical malpractice or product liability.

Our total cumulative liability hereunder in connection with this book, if any, are limited to the fees received for the purchase of a single book specifically relating to the end-user's use of the book which is the subject of the claim. Nothing in these terms and conditions will: (a) limit or exclude our or your liability for death or personal injury resulting from negligence; (b) limit or exclude our or your liability for fraud or fraudulent misrepresentation; (c) limit any of our or your liabilities in any way that is not permitted under applicable law; or (d) exclude any of our or your liabilities that may not be excluded under applicable law.

By reading this content, you accept and agree to the aforementioned in full.

ACKNOWLEDGMENTS

Thank-you Naomi for being such a beautiful, amazing, loving
person.
I love you and am so proud of you, today and forever.

DEDICATION

In loving memory of Randy.

TABLE OF CONTENTS

Preface

Where to Start

In February of 2016 I published my first book, which was called 'A Prescription for Alcoholics–Medications for Alcoholism', and which I refer to here as the 'original book.'

It was the first book ever published to extensively cover an entire category of medications–FDA-approved medications–that have been proven effective in the treatment of alcoholism.

It also provided information about how to access the medication and get treatment, as well as providing detailed medical information about how alcoholism works in the brain.

I'm lucky enough to be able to say that I have never struggled with an addiction myself. Instead, my research was inspired by my friend Randy's battle with alcoholism, which I wrote about extensively in the original book.

The book you are reading now is part of the 4-book series that has emerged from the content of that original book.

Much of the content here was initially published in Part 1 of the original book. But it was a very long book, spanning over 550 pages, and covering a lot of topics! Perhaps there was too much information for many readers to wade through.

But now, by dividing the original book into four volumes, I hope to make the extensive information I collected even more accessible to anyone that needs it.

The primary goal of the original book was to let people know about the valid, well-researched pharmaceutical treatments that can help someone with alcoholism reduce or quit drinking.

Despite the enormous amount of scientific evidence supporting its effectiveness, as well as its endorsement at the most senior levels of US government, Medication Assisted Treatment (MAT) of alcoholism is rarely offered to alcoholics.

It is even more rarely offered to individuals who sense a problem on the horizon and are seeking help to reduce or quit drinking before it becomes a major health problem.

This means that the likelihood of any reader of this book walking into their doctor's office and walking out with an appropriate prescription and medical support to help them reduce drinking on the very first try is extremely low. Doctors are simply unaware of the importance of these medications or how to prescribe them properly.

So for anyone beginning their medication journey, the content you'll find here will be invaluable in helping you to navigate the system so that you have the best chance of obtaining the right support and care.

Much of the content here was initially published in Part 3 of the first book. But the first book was very large and covered a lot of topics! Perhaps too many for many readers to wade through.

But now, by dividing the original book into several parts (some of which are still to be published), I hope to make the extensive information contained in the first book even more accessible to anyone that needs it.

Here is short summary of what each book in the new series covers:

Book 1: The AA Effect & Why You've Never Heard of the FDA-Approved Drugs that Treat Alcoholism

Start here if you'd like to know why you may never have heard of these medications before and what needs to change so alcoholics start receiving proper medical care.

In Book 1 we also look at the roles of the 'players' in the system–doctors, pharmaceutical companies, 12-step groups (AA) and more.

We are taken through a journey of where we've been, where we are, and what we need to do next. It also explains more about why I research and write about this topic.

Book 2: How Alcoholism Works in the Brain

Start here if you'd like a better understanding of the brain disease called alcoholism.

This book includes an in-depth explanation of how alcoholism works inside the brain; the stages of alcoholism identified by researchers; and a list of clues to your genetic vulnerability.

If you haven't thought about alcoholism from a true medical perspective before, this book may be of help to you.

Book 3: Reduce or Stop Drinking with Medication – The How-To Guide

If you are considering taking medication to treat alcoholism, but are wondering where to begin, start with this book–Book 3.

You'll learn everything you need to know to obtain treatment with medication including finding a doctor and obtaining medication.

This book includes information on determining goals, tracking results, developing a medication strategy, combining medications, determining what type of alcoholism you may have, how to obtain medication, and many other considerations.

Book 4: Medications to Reduce or Quit Drinking – The Drug Compendium

Start here if you would like in-depth information about specific medications and the research that backs them up. This book contains invaluable research, insights and links to additional resources that will help you and your doctor to determine which medications are right for you. There is also an important section covering drugs (some of them very common), which may cause some people to actually increase their drinking.

Here you'll find over 200 pages of detailed, meticulously researched information on drugs that can treat alcoholism. Highlights from over 300 scientific research reports are referenced and summarized.

This book is divided into four lists:

1) The A-List–Most Important Medications Today

2) The B-List–Medications Worth Consideration Today

3) The D-List–Eleven Drugs that May Increase Drinking

4) The Futures List–Sixty+ Drugs to Watch

I encourage you to photocopy sections of Book 4 to bring to your doctor, and also visit the book's website (APrescriptionForAlcoholics.com) to access and print the most important research highlighted for each medication.

Spread the Word

If this book has made a difference to you, please consider helping to spread the word.

You can do this by:

- Sharing a free chapter found on the website with a friend (www.APrescriptionforAlcoholics.com)

- Passing the book on to someone you know.

- Donating a few copies to a library, school, doctor's office or recovery program.

- Posting about the book on social media.

01 | HOW THE MEDICATIONS WORK

"Given that many neurotransmitter systems are affected...numerous druggable targets have been identified; consequently, a "cocktail" of different compounds will further improve the treatment situation."[8]

—Dr. Rainer Spanagel, Director of the Institute of Psychopharmacology, University of Heidelberg

HOW MEDICATIONS FOR
ALCOHOLISM WORK

Between environmental contributors, genes and brain neuroadaptation, alcoholism generates a lot of feelings and behaviors that contribute to the development and reinforcement of alcohol dependence.

For example, alcoholism can manifest characteristics that influence alcoholics to:

- be more impulsive

- be less able to halt impulsive, automatic actions

- seek thrills

- experience a strong enjoyment of alcohol

- be highly reactive to alcohol cues

- become drunk more quickly than others

- feel less affected by drinking (dependence)

- experience chronic anxiety, depression or other mental illness

- develop deep conditioned responses more quickly

- react more strongly to stressors

- experience obsessive thoughts and cravings

- feel uninterested in anything but drinking

- have difficulty valuing negative consequences

Some people experience all of these. Some experience few. Everyone is different.

If you were freed from just one of these feelings and behaviors—for example–'chronic anxiety', or if you were only able to remove 'obsessive thoughts and cravings', maybe it would allow you to stop the addiction cycle.

Or, perhaps if every one of these feelings and behaviors remained, but were just lessened by 10%, you would be able to regain control.

Researchers recognize the importance of minimizing these feelings and behaviors, and so in developing medications for alcoholism, researchers look at these feelings and behaviors and try to identify the parts of the brain that are generating them.

All of the characteristics described above are produced inside the brain, and there are many different systems in the brain, such as the dopamine system, and systems that the dopamine system involves, such as glutamate, serotonin, GABA, corticotropin-releasing factor, and opioid that are involved in generating them.

Knowing that these systems are involved in alcoholism, researchers try to identify drug compounds (existing or new ones) that target these systems.

And by targeting and interfering with these systems, researchers hope to interfere with the thoughts and feelings that contribute to alcoholism.

For example, let's look at one target–the opioid system.

We know that the opioid system (part of the reward system which is related to feel-good endorphins), is involved in the reinforcing effects of alcohol.

We also know that there are variations in at least four genes that are related to the opioid system that are found in alcoholic populations.

For example, OPRM1 is a gene that is related to at least three opioid receptors in humans. So something is occurring in the opioid system of alcoholics to contribute to their alcoholism, that may not occur in non-alcoholics.

Therefore, for scientists looking for a way to interrupt the addiction process–the behaviors and feelings associated with alcoholism, the opioid system becomes a natural 'target'.

Naltrexone is a drug that is known to interfere with the opioid system.

It binds to opioid receptors, blocking them so that the rewarding feeling of alcohol may be muted. Over time, it can also help reverse the altered balance in the brain, undoing alcohol conditioning.

By undoing conditioning, fewer cravings for alcohol may be experienced.

So, by targeting the opioid system with the medication naltrexone, at least three of the feelings and behaviors associated with alcoholism can be weakened or eradicated:

- experience a strong enjoyment of alcohol
- develop deep conditioned responses more quickly
- experience obsessive thoughts and cravings

Whether for depression, Alzheimer's, or alcoholism, targeting brain systems is an imprecise science.

It's generally known which systems a drug is interfering with, but not what the outcome of the interference will be.

And when the outcome is good (for example, by reducing craving), researchers don't necessarily even understand why the drug is working.

That's why, for many of the medicines used to target excessive drinking, the 'mechanism of action', or in other words, how the drug actually works, is nothing more than an extremely well-educated guess.

You'll notice that naltrexone may be helpful with three feelings and behaviors associated with alcoholism and the reward system.

But how about all of the other feelings and characteristics?

Others may be more a result of issues in other brain systems, and so these other brain systems become another 'target' for researchers, and drugs that are designed to interfere with these targets can be applied.

While the numerous targets make alcoholism very complex, it also means lots of opportunity.

As scientists wrote in one journal article in 2013, "there is no other field in psychiatric research that has, in recent years, yielded so many novel, druggable targets and innovative treatment strategies than for alcohol addiction."[8]

CAUSES OF ADDICTION VERSUS DAMAGE CAUSED BY ADDICTION

As you are thinking about the behaviors and feelings that contribute to your alcoholism or over-drinking, it may be helpful to think about how you felt when your drinking was first developing, and how you feel now. These can be valuable clues to help you understand what you need to tackle.

For example, did you drink routinely and heavily because you were trying to manage stress or anxiety? Or did you do so because drinking was so enjoyable?

And now that you are drinking more than you want to, what is it that you feel before you relapse? Severe cravings? Anxiety? Or perhaps you don't sense cravings, but seem to automatically just head for the bottle.

The more you understand how your own brain and body is being motivated and affected, the better chance you will have of choosing medications that might help you.

For example, whereas the rewards of thrill- and sensation-seeking may have driven you to overdrink in the first place, it might be a state of anxiety, stress, and depression caused by the addiction that now contributes to each consecutive relapse.

One is related to causal factors, and the other is related to the chronic damage caused by the disease. For these two separate dimensions, different treatments may be appropriate.[1]

Multi-prong strategies may be very necessary, involving various types of treatments and combinations of treatments (pharmaceutical and other), which target multiple goals.[9]

Some of these treatment and medication goals which include a variety of different areas and systems of the brain, and might target both the causes and the chronic effects of alcoholism might include a "cocktail of compounds"[8] involved in:

- decreasing the reward value of the drug

- increasing the reward value of non-drug reinforcers

- weakening conditioned drug behaviors and motivators

- decreasing obsession and craving

- strengthening frontal inhibitory and executive control

- reducing reactivity to stressors

SHORT CIRCUITING ADDICTION

Every now and then a major discovery is made that throws other discoveries before it into question (or solves their mysteries), as well as paving the way for new insights and treatments.

In 2007 such a discovery was made: Scientists studying stroke patients realized that an injury to the insula could instantly and permanently break a smoking habit.[10]

The Director of the National Institute on Drug Abuse (Dr. George Koob) said of the discovery, "This is the first time we've shown anything like this, that damage to a specific brain area could remove the problem of addiction entirely...It's absolutely mind-boggling."[10]

Scientists knew that the insula was a structure in the brain that was involved in addiction, but they had no idea just how important it was.

It is still a mysterious and complex part of the brain, nicknamed by one researcher as the 'hidden island of addiction' and related to highly evolved processes.

It is thought to "integrate introceptive states into conscious feelings and into decision-making processes that involve uncertain risk and reward." It seems to be related to the experience of craving and intuition.[11]

Researchers found that patients with damage to the insula underwent a complete disruption of smoking addiction which was:

> "*...characterized by the ability to quit smoking easily, immediately, without relapse and without a persistence of the urge to smoke.*
>
> *In one case, this disruption of addiction after insula damage was so profound as to lead one patient to proclaim that his 'body forgot the urge to smoke.'*"[11]

In other words, damage to the insula eradicated the addiction to smoking. No behavioral therapy, soul searching, fighting of urges and cravings was necessary–through damage to the insula, smoking addiction was simply wiped out.

How is this related to alcoholism?

I'm not recommending you go out and try to injure your insula.

While being an important discovery on many other levels, what the discovery shows is that alcohol addiction researchers are on the right track when it comes to targeting the brain's biology.

It provides validity to the notion that irrespective of the environment you grew up in or the psychological baggage you carry, if changes to a specific section of the brain in an addicted smoker can extinguish addiction, then it can be achieved (maybe through a different mechanism, or a different area), in alcoholics too.

Dr. Koob is correct when he says that this is the first time we've seen anything like this–in that this experiment showed such a profound and complete reversal of addiction in nearly every insula injury.

However, this phenomena has also been seen in alcoholics taking specific medications too.

For example, in the treatment he developed and tested on himself using baclofen, Dr. Olivier Amiesen describes a 'switch'–a point at which addiction is 'turned off' in treatment.

When Amiesen (and many others since) experienced this switch point, their experience was one in which the intense craving for alcohol one day simply disappeared.

Other individuals, such as many for whom naltrexone has been successful, have experienced the same effect–that eventually at a point in their treatment, they simply no longer feel the extreme obsession and drive to drink and inability to stop, any more.

02 | THREE TREATMENT STEPS

"So with no other disease do we expect people to wait until they're a danger to themselves or others to self-diagnose and seek treatment.

Every other disease — you got a broken leg, you got diabetes, you got some sort of sickness, we understand that we got to get you help.

And we also understand when it comes to other diseases that if we don't give you help, and let you suffer by yourself, then other people could get sick.

Well, this is an illness. And we got to treat it, as such. We have to change our mindset."[12]

—US President Barack Obama

STEP 1: GETTING PREPARED

If you didn't read the legal statements early in this book, please go back and read it now. It contains important information that you should not read further without.

GOALS & GOAL TRACKING

ABSTINENCE OR REDUCTION

> *"If an addict has made major advances, taken steps in positive directions that few would argue with, then it is absurd to suggest that this person is not recovering. A switch from 10 bottles or 10 bags a week to 2 bottles or 2 bags a week is a huge improvement and obviously should qualify as 'recovery'."*[13]

What would you like your treatment goal to be?

Your goal will impact which medications you choose to take and even how you decide to take them.

Let's step back and talk first about the goals now available for treatment.

•••

There is a significant shift in perspective occurring in our thinking around what a treatment goal can and should be for someone with alcoholism.

If you have been in treatment or in a 12-step program, you may believe that the only possible goal is abstinence. And perhaps that still is the best goal for you. (Or maybe it never was a realistic goal for you, and never will be).

Abstinence is the very black and white goal that AA has laid out for alcoholics.

And for people in the program, even status and tenure are measured on the basis of that goal–one day at a time.

Anniversaries of sobriety–1 day, 1 month, 1 year–and more are hard won and celebrated. Fall off the wagon and you start again at day 1. Sobriety or nothing–there is no middle ground–'cutting down' counts for nada.

Unfortunately, abstinence simply doesn't work as a treatment option for many people with this disease. If you are one of them, then another goal maybe more realistic for you.

Abstinence from alcohol works about as well for many as abstinence from sex works as a form of birth control–a nice idea but not very practical. And as with AA's philosophy of abstinence, it's an idea from an earlier time.

HARM REDUCTION

For people who are not interested in a solution that involves abstinence, there are other options.

These options are categorized under the term 'harm reduction', or simply 'reduction'. Many organizations and support groups espouse this approach that can be found by simply searching for 'alcohol harm reduction' online. One example can be found at hamsnetwork.org, ("Where better is better!")

Harm reduction strategies are aimed at reducing the negative consequences associated with alcohol dependence.

This is an important approach to the treatment of a progressive disease that is often fatal.

ABSTINENCE GOALS: A BARRIER TO TREATMENT?

One of the reasons that people do not pursue treatment is because in the past treatment has *always* meant abstinence.

Heavy drinkers (often with the greatest risk of harm from alcoholism) often desperately want the option of moderating their drinking if they can, instead of trying to give it up altogether.[14]

The black and white 'abstinence or nothing' approach is a major barrier to helping alcoholics. In one study 50% of those who knew they needed it did not seek treatment because they were not ready to give up alcohol.[15]

This is worth repeating—half of the people who knew they needed help did not get it because they were not prepared to stop drinking. They were not ready for any treatment that had abstinence as a goal.

These are the people who desperately need treatment options that help them to decrease their consumption.

Another reason people don't pursue treatment is because of the perception that treatment means involvement in a program.

The following are additional reasons why people who knew they needed help did not seek it (numbers rounded).[15] Notice how each one is related to an element of program participation:

- No transportation/inconvenient—7%
- No program having type of treatment—8%
- No openings in a program—1%
- Did not know where to go for treatment—7%
- Might cause community to have negative opinion—6%
- Might have negative effect on job—7%

- Did not have time–3%

- Did not want others to find out–2%

In total, 43% of individuals who knew they needed help for their alcohol dependence did not get it because of issues around program participation.[15]

Again–worth repeating–43 percent of the people who knew they needed help did not get it because of issues likely related to participating in a program.

These are the people who–even if they *are* willing to accept abstinence as a goal–will not receive any treatment for their illness if the solution is program-based.

But as with those who aren't willing to give up drinking, for these program-averse people, medication (confidential, non-time consuming, non-participatory), is an option that they might be open to.

For those individuals, if only one medication is tried, and that medication was effective for only one in three individuals (the 'number needed to treat' for baclofen), that would mean that one in three people could see improvement in a disease that they would otherwise not be getting treatment for—one which could otherwise be progressively killing them.

The president of pharmaceutical company Lundbeck (Ulf Wiinberg) reiterates this perspective. Lundbeck has launched the 'as needed' medication Selincro in Europe that is targeted toward individuals seeking a reduction in consumption.

He says, "If we can get addicts to reduce their consumption from 50-100 drinks a week to 20-25, then we will have come a long way. In this way, these people could regain control of their own lives. This would be a viable solution for certain groups of users."[16]

Is 'Reduction' a Naïve Goal?

Is treatment that only aims for a reduction in consumption naïve?

For some people, it may be just the opposite. As researchers point out–it is not *drinking* that causes so many health problems for alcoholics–it's *heavy drinking* that leads to the burden of disease and cost associated with alcoholism.[17]

Therefore, if heavy drinking can be reduced to moderate drinking, many lives could be saved. For example, research shows that:

- For an alcoholic drinking 8 glasses of alcohol per day, if he reduces his intake by just 2 glasses per day, his one-year mortality risk is nearly cut in half.[18]

- In heavy drinkers (those who drink 100g or more per day), cutting consumption in half reduces the chance of death by 800%.[17]

Given these statistics, it's hard to understand why there was not a focus on using medication to help alcoholics reduce consumption, years ago. Why *wouldn't* we look for ways to reduce consumption if we could?

Clearly, reduction is not a naïve approach—especially given that the alternative for many is not abstinence–but simply continued drinking at high levels.

Reduction can also be an intermediate step in the right direction for those who eventually choose abstinence as a goal.

There are many anecdotal stories from people who have taken medications and been able to reduce their drinking, and who, once they were able to cut down, decided that abstinence was possible and preferable for them.

ABSTINENCE CAN BE DANGEROUS

The idea that abstinence (from alcohol as well as medical assistance) is the only definition of true recovery is not only old but, more importantly, it's outdated–and dangerous.

In a study of 1800 treated drinkers done in 2007 that looked at the aftermath of treatment which focused on abstinence versus moderation, they found that individuals that chose abstinence experienced negative consequences (due to drinking, or relapsing), at the same rate as individuals whose goal had been to moderate drinking.[14]

Other research on the Abstinence Violation Effect has shown that when an alcoholic believes a lapse is a shameful and devastating personal failure (as the abstinence philosophy implies), they are much more likely to continue to a full-blown binge, instead of stopping and regrouping.[19]

SHIFTING PHILOSOPHY

Thankfully, the 'all-or-nothing medication-free abstinence' approach is slowly starting to come under fire in the US, but North America is lagging behind Europe in this way of thinking.

Recent research shows that in Europe at least, "many clinicians and patients consider reduction of alcohol consumption as a valuable treatment option to reduce the consequences of harmful alcohol use or, at least, as an intermediate goal towards abstinence, and research evidence supports this."[20]

And the European Medicines Agency (equivalent to the US FDA) has guidelines that recognize both treatment goals: abstinence and reduction in alcohol consumption.

Practitioners and patients are starting to recognize reduction as a viable goal. And even the tone of articles and government reports indicate a subtle undercurrent that a "philosophy of abstinence" may not, and should not, be for everyone.

What This Means For You

Once you have thought about and determined what your goal is, this will help you (and your medical advisor) to choose which medications to try.

As you read the information about each drug in Book 4 of this series, you'll see information on each one regarding the goals the medication might assist you with.

For example, if your goal is abstinence, you will want to avoid any medication (or more accurately—any *methods* of taking that medication) on an 'as needed' basis. Alcohol consumption is a key component of the science behind 'as needed' methods. (You can take 'as needed' medications and abstain too, but you'll be following a different method. As this is confusing, see the naltrexone section in Book 4 for a detailed explanation).

Perhaps you can seek medications that help with your trigger points instead–such as those that have been seen to address strong cravings, anxiety, or alcohol cue reactivity.

If your goal is a reduction in drinking, most of the medications written about in Book 4 are an option for you.

Nalmefene is an example of a drug that is taken 'as needed'– meaning it is taken an hour before drinking–to help reduce drinking.

Therefore, abstinence isn't its (initial) goal.

Naltrexone and topiramate are two other medications known for their ability to help reduce drinking.

TRACKING

"What gets measured gets managed."

–Peter Drucker

Tracking important measures helps us manage many illnesses.

For example, if you have type 1 diabetes, doctors recommend that you check your blood sugar four to eight times per day. Blood pressure is another metric commonly measured to manage disease.

Not everyone is good at tracking–it takes a certain amount of discipline to do so–and courage to look at the numbers when they may not be as good as we would like.

But, as with other diseases, if you have alcohol dependence and track the amount you drink, it may help you manage this disease too.

Tracking will help you see whether what you are doing is helping, or if another strategy should be considered.

If you bring your data to your doctor, it will also help your doctor see that you are committed to change. It may help them get on board with you on your journey–something that will be extremely valuable to you if you are going to go down the path of experimenting to see if one or more medications can help you.

Two metrics are commonly measured by people who are tracking their consumption:

- Number of drinks per day

- Number of drink-free days

Also, if you find that these are factors in your drinking, and really want to diligently track your progress or triggers, you could also track (on a scale of 1 to 10) any of the following:

- The amount of craving you are experiencing

- The amount of stress you are experiencing

- The amount of anxiety you are experiencing

People track using different tools.

For example:

- A notebook you carry with you (a 'drinking diary')

- A simple notepad app on a cell phone

- By taking a photo with your phone of each drink you start, and counting later

- A cell phone app that is specifically used for measuring drinking

There are quite a few cell phone apps now available–some of which are free, and some of which cost a few dollars.

Using an app can help take away the problem of determining whether drinks are equivalent or not.

For example, if I drink four glasses of wine today, and four bottles of beer tomorrow, did I drink the same amount each day? Yes, I drank the same number of drinks, but certainly not the same amount of alcohol.

Some apps can help you compare apples to apples by allowing you to categorize drinks as you enter them, and then letting the app determine actual alcohol consumption.

A quick search online for cell phone apps found:

- AlcoDroid Alcohol Tracker

- SoberApp Alcohol Calculator

- My Daily Journal

- Drinking Buddy

- DrinkControl

If it sounds like a lot of work—well maybe it is—but have you ever redecorated a room and wished you had taken a 'before' picture before you started?

Tracking your drinking is like that. If you are able to reduce your consumption, there is a great deal of reward gained when you can see the numbers go down. It may take weeks or months for that to happen, but when it does, you'll be glad that you tracked.

In some of the online forums mentioned later, people anonymously post their drinking diary data (sometimes in their signature, so it appears after every posting), and update them daily or once a week.

Here's an example of how this looks.

The first number represents the number of drinks per week, and the second represents the number of 'Alcohol Free' ('AF') days the individual experienced:

Week 1—25—1 AF

Week 2—41—0 AF

Week 3—40—0 AF

Week 4—52—0 AF

Week 5—37—0 AF

Week 6—37—0 AF

Week 7—37—1 AF

Week 8—24—3 AF

Seeing other people's diaries is motivating—you can see that for some people medication works very quickly, while for others, it take a long time to work (if it ever works). It helps to know other people are in the same boat, and you aren't alone.

And if you decide to track and post your drinking diary in a forum too, you may be surprised at the encouragement you receive from others in your journey.

YOUR MEDICAL TREATMENT OPTIONS

WHAT TO EXPECT FROM YOUR DOCTOR

What should you expect from your doctor?

Nothing. You should be prepared to be underwhelmed, unfortunately.

When you start to talk to your doctor about pharmaceutical treatment for your alcoholism, you may suddenly feel like you are Alice in Wonderland.

This is because you might find yourself in a situation where you will be asking him or her for:

- Medical Treatment for a medical condition

- FDA-approved medication that has been used safely for decades

- Medication in large enough doses to treat your condition

- Treatment protocols for dosing that are backed by published research by respected scientists.

Not much to ask for really.

And yet, you may find that he or she:

- Has never heard of either the medications or treatments you are referencing and won't take your request seriously;

- Suggests that you go to a 12-step religion-based program like AA (with no medical/scientific evidence backing it);

- Might haltingly be convinced to prescribe you with the medication you are seeking, but in much lower doses than the effective (proven) dosages.

Welcome to Wonderland.

When it comes to medical, pharmacological treatment of alcohol addiction, you and I are pioneers and most (but not all) doctors are still back in 1939 with Bill Wilson. So be prepared.

Imagine if you went in with diabetes and asked for proper treatment and he/she responded in the same way—told you go find your higher power and dismissed your request for treatment? It might be lawsuit time.

We are just in a very different place in the treatment of alcoholism. Know it, be prepared for it, and don't take no for an answer—don't be another tragedy in the making.

If your doctor positively responds to all your requests on the first try, then you are seeing one of a small handful of very rare, very enlightened doctors in the world. Congratulations. You are incredibly lucky! With their support and cooperation, you have a strong chance of actually making life with this disease much more manageable.

If and when you are lucky enough to obtain some of the medications written about in this book you will be on a new path. Not just new to you—new to the world.

This pathway can be very challenging—managing side effects, wondering whether anything is working, experimenting with correct dosages and combinations. Again—unless you are incredibly lucky—your doctor won't be much help to you in these areas.

But please—don't confuse your doctor's lack of knowledge as meaning that these medical options are not excellent, effective, life-changing medical treatments…your doctor just doesn't have experience with them, education about them, or colleagues who have more expertise than themselves in this area.

There are many resources mentioned in this book series where you can learn much more about treatments and what to expect than your family physician will ever be able to offer you. Use those resources.

Manage your own recovery and research, and you will soon know much more about the treatment of alcoholism than your doctor will.

And you can (and probably will) be the first of your doctor's patients to go through this process, which means you'll be helping to train your doctor and make treatment easier for every other patient that comes after you. You can help save the lives of people you'll never meet in this way.

If your doctor won't work with you to find a solution using medications in this book, then what are your options?

You have a few.

Each of your options are discussed a little later. You might not like all of them. I'm not telling you to do any of them–all I want for you is to know your options and manage your health with your own best interests in mind.

Try to Manage Your Doctor

Do your best to attempt to nurture a partnership with your doctor.

He/she might just hold the keys to your illness in their hand. See this as a business partnership if you can and help guide your doctor to the knowledge that can help them help you. For example:

- Print out relevant parts of this book and Book 4, print some of the research that is referenced in Book 4, and something similar to the letter below. You may want to drop it all off in advance.

- Book time with your doctor for a talk.

- Dress and act as professionally as possible. If you have the means, try to wear what you would wear to a business meeting. Appearance makes a difference. It shouldn't. It does.

- Book time when you will be at your most lucid and sober.

- Bring a friend who can help advocate for you.

- Search online for "how to advocate with your doctor" for tips and ideas.

- There are ways to speak with your doctor that will help guide them in the direction you wish to go. Learn about these and practice them. For example, "I found this on the internet" might not be a good start, but "a doctor at the addiction treatment center recommended I look into this," may keep them listening to you for longer.

- Be relentless. It's your life and your health–not theirs.

Start with a First Line Drug

If your doctor has little experience with treating alcoholism with medication, then this may be a critical piece of advice for you: start out with a first line drug.

A first line drug will be far more within your doctor's comfort zone than other drugs.

A 'first line' treatment is usually the first 'go-to' medication that a doctor might prescribe for a medical condition. (Though, in the treatment of alcoholism, very few people are ever prescribed any pharmaceutical treatment, so this term is something of a misnomer here).

Whether a medication is first or second line is subjective. This designation reflects both the effectiveness of the medication, but perhaps more so it simply reflects the length of time that doctors have prescribed the drug, thus building a level of confidence in its safety.

A medication can be highly effective and not be considered a first or second line treatment–particularly if the medical community has not been prescribing it for any length of time.

Even if the first line medication does not work for you, it's possible that by starting with these medications you can start a partnership with your doctor on your journey, and maybe they will feel more confident about prescribing you another medication that is a second or third line treatment.

Acamprosate and naltrexone are both first line drugs that are great starting points because they are the only two drugs on the A-List in Book 4 that are FDA-approved for the treatment of alcoholism in most places in the world.

Nalmefene is a good place to start if you are in Europe (and may be considered first line there) because it was recently launched there for alcoholism treatment and there is substantial pharmaceutical marketing creating a push for it with doctors right now. (It's not available in North America though). Lundbeck has placed some excellent resources online for physicians that can get them up to speed on the medication.

Baclofen is a first line drug and a good starting point for people in France because it was recently approved there to be prescribed specifically for the treatment of alcoholism. Doctors have more familiarity with baclofen in France for alcoholism treatment than they do in North America or other parts of Europe.

By starting with any of these, you won't be asking your doctor to prescribe you a medication for alcoholism that was approved for another medical condition (an 'off-label' medication).

All four—baclofen, naltrexone, nalmefene and acamprosate—are quite effective in some individuals, and there is a large body of research evidence you can bring to your doctor to back up each of these choices.

Most doctors who have heard of or prescribed any medication for alcoholism will start with disulfiram, and consider it to be the very first first line drug to prescribe.

If you are just starting out, read up carefully on this medication (it's on the B-List in Book 4), as there are some good reasons (that your doctor may not know about) *not* to start with this one.

Look for another Doctor

If you simply can't convince your doctor to work with you on this, then you may need to look for another doctor.

Here are a few things to keep in mind:

- Research doctors online–see if you can learn anything about their flexibility and accommodation in working with their patients in other areas.

  Online reviews can tell you a lot about a doctor's approach in general. For example, I've never asked my doctor for medication for alcoholism, but I know that when I have researched medications for other issues, if I bring her information about it, she will consider it for me and work with me. She is neither arrogant, nor dismissive. She is patient and open to new ideas, especially if those ideas are backed by credible research.

  These are the traits to look for in online reviews, and if you have several options to choose from, doctors who are unwilling to consider a well-versed patient's input are doctors you may wish to avoid.

- Some forums (links are later in the book) provide lists of doctors that are known to treat alcoholism with medication. You could also post a question on a forum asking for recommendations in your area. Or you could choose to travel a little farther to a doctor who has been identified as knowledgeable.

It may be well worth your time to travel a few hours in order to see a doctor with experience in this area and who is willing to work with you.

- If you find a new doctor (especially a new one that may not have experience with alcohol medication, but who you think may exhibit traits you are looking for), you may wish to build a relationship with the new doctor first with a few visits for some other minor issue.

Be profession, reliable, credible and build a rapport with them. Sadly alcoholism is still stigmatized. It's unfair, but a doctor may be more likely to see you as a credible human being if you don't initially present yourself as having an addiction problem.

WHAT TO BRING TO YOUR DOCTOR

Book 4 of this series was written to help you learn the most important information about each medication, but also so that you would have research and medical information to bring to your doctor when you discuss the drugs with him or her.

The information about each drug has been written in the order in which it would be most useful to a doctor to read.

Each of the drug sections in Book 4 will provide the following:

- A paragraph or two introducing some of the key facts about the medication;

- A Q&A section that answers many of the most important things you and your doctor need to know about each medication as possible;

- A list of significant research and the main findings of each piece of research in order of most recent to oldest.

- A little more background information about the drug that may be of interest to some.

- Thoughts and comments from alcoholics who have experience taking the medication.

You may wish to photocopy and bring the entire section on the medication or medications you are interested in. Please feel free to do so.

You may also want to look up and print out the most recent research that is referenced in sections that cover each medication. All of the resources listed there would be appropriate and even quite useful to give to a doctor and many can be found from the book website, www.APrescriptionforAlcoholics.com.

Bring a professional-looking package with you and be prepared to drop it off a week or two in advance of the appointment or leave it behind for the doctor to review.

The following is a letter you may wish to include. You could include a photocopy of it, with a handwritten note from yourself.

Your note could say something like, "Looking forward to our appointment at 3 on Thursday the 7th. I'm hoping that we can discuss my options with one of these medications. Perhaps something of interest here." Or something to that effect.

LETTER TO YOUR DOCTOR

Dear Doctor,

Your patient would like your help in the treatment of their alcohol dependence.

While it may not be widely known, there are several prescription medications that can help reduce craving, increase the time to relapse and reduce drinking quantity.

These drugs include: naltrexone, acamprosate (both approved by FDA, Health Canada and European Medicines Agency for the treatment of alcohol dependence); as well as baclofen, topiramate, nalmefene, gabapentin, ondansetron, sertraline, prazosin/doxazosin, varenicline and zonisamide (all widely approved off-label; baclofen approved on-label for alcohol dependence in France and nalmefene approved on-label for alcohol dependence in Europe).

Your patient has an interest in one or more of these medications and has brought additional information to you that it's hoped will be of assistance to you in determining whether or not the medication is appropriate.

In the interest of evidence-based medicine, and so you can determine the best approach, the information brought by your patient includes a list of significant research findings for the medication(s) of interest, general information about the medication, as well as a list of relevant research reports.

You can access the research reports (or their abstracts) at the website associated with this book which contains links to each journal article mentioned. Or simply search for them on Google Scholar (scholar.google.com).

Thank-you for your support and for the incredibly important role you play.

And thank-you in advance for taking time from your busy schedule to carefully read and review the information provided.

Sincerely,

Your Patient

THREE OTHER OPTIONS

Some people have found that no matter how they approach their doctor, they cannot succeed in obtaining medical treatment from within their own healthcare system for their dependence on alcohol.

Individuals who have come up to a brick wall have found some other options. These include:

1) Seeking medical treatment outside their own country;

2) Seeking treatment for a different illness that is treated with the same medications; and/or

3) Purchasing medication themselves without a prescription via an online pharmacy.

NOBODY in this century, living in any first world country, should need to resort to any of these options. People (particularly the same doctors that won't prescribe you the medications in this book) will call them dangerous. I think some of them are dangerous. I don't think that anyone should feel that in order to save their own lives they must resort to any of these options.

But as I discussed in earlier books in this series, there is a treatment gap that 20.7 million alcoholics in the United States are falling into.[3]

Authorities say, "there simply is no other disease where appropriate medical treatment is not provided by the health care system."[3]

And the Director of the Harvard Medical School says, "there is no other comparable example in medicine where you have evidence-based treatments that are not available.[3] (In other words, they are available, but not to you.)

So that sterile waiting room at your doctor's office may look like it's from this century; your doctor's education may be the best training there is; there may be a cutting edge computer sitting on the office desk.

But in some cases, you may as well be sitting in Doc Baker's Walnut Grove office from Little House on the Prairie for all the help you'll receive.

What's more dangerous—taking matters into your own hands for a disease that can destroy your life and kill you? Or sitting in a 'treatment gap' in your doctor's office waiting for help that never comes?

Option 1: Leave the Country

One approach that some individuals take is to cross the border to the 'border-town' clinics and pharmacies that exist for that purpose in some countries.

If, for example, you live in Canada, and wish to obtain naltrexone by monthly injection (not yet approved in Canada), then one approach some people take is to travel across the border to the United States once a month to obtain the injection there. (One bonus of this option is that because it's an injection you won't be bringing medication back into the country). [Note: Since I published the original book I have learned that there are also 6-month injection options—so you may only need to visit twice a year.]

Disulfiram is no longer approved by the government in Canada so those looking for it may need to go to a compounding pharmacy (a pharmacy that will literally make the medication for you). But an alternative may be to obtain it in the United States instead.

If you are outside, but close to France, it may be somewhere you could visit to obtain medical supervision for baclofen.

Nalmefene is currently only available in parts of Europe and is another medication that might be more easily obtained from cross-border visits to parts of Europe.

'Medical tourism' is a big industry–many people plan trips to other parts of the world to obtain medical treatment and prescriptions there.

Of course, if you go outside your country, buyer beware. Be careful and cautious. The same principles you'd apply to every other area of your health applies here too.

Be cautious and don't break the law.

Do your research, no matter where you go.

And make sure you know the rules for bringing medications back across the border before you take the trip. It may be wise to look at shipping medication over the border to yourself instead of trying to carry them back (but again–make sure the approach you take is legal).

You can contact the customs office for the country you will be exiting and re-entering, to find out specific rules for what you can and cannot bring across the border.

Option 2: Seek Treatment for a Different Illness

I'm not advocating that you seek treatment for a different illness– I'm just reporting here on what others have done.

Many medications identified in Book 4 are commonly prescribed and FDA approved for other purposes. Many doctors are very comfortable prescribing them for those other purposes.

For example, topiramate is often prescribed for migraines (and sometimes prescribed for weight-loss) and varenicline is widely known as a smoking cessation treatment.

Sometimes, for some people, if faced with not receiving any kind of treatment or medical supervision at all (and all other avenues are exhausted), this is the only option they are left with.

Option 3: Treat Yourself

Some individuals have successfully found overseas pharmacies which will provide them with a prescription and will ship medication to them, thus completely bypassing their physician.

I estimate that a significant percentage of people (perhaps 20-50%) writing about their experiences with these medications within forums obtain the medication they are using from online pharmacies.

Some online pharmacies require a prescription from a doctor to be provided to them before they will ship the order.

Others will allow you to pay a little extra for an assessment by a pharmacy-employed doctor who will then provide a prescription for the medication.

One reputable online pharmacy that I have ordered from provides an online assessment, so that the individual placing the order never interacts with or speaks to a physician before the prescription is made.

There are many scams on the internet, and many people that will gladly take your money or steal your identity and give you nothing in return. Some of these scams involve online pharmacies.

Please be very cautious if you take this approach. Order only a very small amount if you are trying a place for the first time. Get a more savvy friend to help you if you can. And attempt to get a recommendation from someone you have developed trust with on an online forum about reputable places to order online medications.

However, if you consider yourself quite internet-savvy and have run out of other viable options, many of the medications in this book can be purchased successfully and cost-effectively from online pharmacies.

I have personally purchased liquid baclofen, baclofen tablets, topiramate and naltrexone at a lower cost, with fewer hassles, than I would have been able to buy it in my country, and had it shipped to a delivery address with few problems.

I did notice that one of the packages was held up at customs, and that in some cases the medication took much longer to arrive than a typical online purchase would. So if you go this route make sure you err strongly on the side of caution if you need to order repeat medications so that you do not run out. Allow yourself at least a month, if not longer, for a shipment.

It is much easier to purchase from online pharmacies if you live in the United States than from Canada, so if you have an address or friends with an address in the United States, this may be an easier alternative for Canadians. (Most, but not all online pharmacies *do not* ship to Canada).

If you run into problems with side effects, go to your doctor immediately and be honest about taking any medications you think may be causing them. These are serious medications that can have some rare, but real side-effects that can harm you.

If you choose this route, be an educated consumer–read everything you can about the medication you are considering taking and be aware of all drug interactions, black label warnings, and side effects before you begin. Be smart and do your research.

DRUGS AND THERAPY

The term 'Medication Assisted Treatment' subtly implies that there is something else besides medication being implemented in treatment.

This subtle suggestion is probably more about positioning (with psychiatrists, counselors, treatment providers and 12-steppers) than anything grounded in science.

Nearly everyone can benefit from 'Assistance', in the form of therapy or counselling. And certainly patients need a great deal more support than they are getting from their medical providers today.

However, from a purely evidence-based perspective, of the hundreds of research reports I read, there was not a single one that showed there was a *conclusive* and *significant* difference in outcome if the medication was paired with intensive therapy or counselling of any kind.

Some, such as Cognitive Behavioral Therapy (CBT) have been shown to be complimentary, but therapy is by no means a critical success factor in Medication Assisted Treatment.

I think as you read the research you'll notice too, that it's the 'Medication', with less emphasis on the 'Assisted' part of Medication Assisted Treatment that is the critical component here.

DEALING WITH NAYSAYERS & THE CRUTCH

BE READY TO BE TOLD NOT TO BOTHER

We live in a culture with a very skewed perspective on the disease of alcoholism.

I've written about that extensively in Book 1, but if you haven't read it, all you need to know is that you may run up against a lot of people in positions of authority (at treatment centres, in the medical system, social workers, nurses, doctors, treatment professionals, etc.), that are under the influence of this skewed perspective and will not be supportive of your efforts to be treated medically.

If you start to go down the path of considering or trying medications, be ready for what you will hear from others.

People don't know about these drugs and the 'AA Effect' has really biased society away from anything that is not 12-step based.

Talk to enough people, and you *will* be told:

- Medication doesn't work

- Medication is a crutch

- Medication is not 'pure sobriety'

- Don't bother

- Medications aren't effective and don't work

- All these medications are addictive

All of these things are entirely untrue.

Please don't listen to them. The people that will tell you certainly haven't read the research and have themselves been immersed in mistruths, maybe for decades.

When asked about medications, here are the kinds of things that people in 'the industry' will say, as quoted from a Newsweek article from 2008 (but you can find this type of sentiment everywhere):

"We need four or five more years to see how [Vivitrol] does," says staff psychiatrist Garrett O'Connor at the Betty Ford Center, in Rancho Mirage, Calif. "And we need to be very cautious, because a failed treatment will set a person back.

The Ford Center and the Hazelden Foundation, in Minnesota, use drugs sparingly, and mostly just in the first days or weeks of recovery, the "detox" phase.

Hazelden will never turn its back on pharmaceutical solutions, but a pill all by itself is not the cure," says William Moyers, Hazelden's vice president of external affairs. "We're afraid that people are seeking a medical route that says treatment is the end, not the beginning."[21]

These kinds of cautious, unfounded responses spread misinformation. They are insidious. They sound like they know what they are talking about, and these people hold senior positions in respected organizations. Why wouldn't you believe them?

But what they say is nonsense. It's fearmongering by 12-step advocates designed to scare anyone considering medications away.

Let's break this down…

Statement:

"We need four or five more years to see how [Vivitrol] does."

Response:

Naltrexone (which is the medication in Vivitrol) has now been researched for over 23 years (since 1992), and the extended release version (Vivitrol), has been studied in humans for over 10 years, since 2005.

And as early as 2002, one report showed that up to 2001 there had already been 14 trials assessing the effectiveness of naltrexone compared with placebo for treating alcoholism, enrolling 2127 subjects, in five countries. It stated, "there is strong evidence that naltrexone significantly reduces alcohol relapses to heavy drinking, the frequency and quantity of alcohol consumption in those who do drink, and alcohol craving."[22]

Highly respected researchers have said:

- "Meta-analyses of available trials, even when the negative study is included in the analysis, unequivocally support NTX [naltrexone injection] efficacy."[1]

- "There is abundant evidence supporting the use of naltrexone for the treatment of alcohol dependence (Level A)."[23]

The first quote comes from Markus Heilig, one of top 10 researchers of alcoholism worldwide; former NIAAA Clinical Director; active medical practitioner; author of more than 200 peer-reviewed journal articles, including papers in Science, PNAS, Lancet, Archives of General Psychiatry. His research work has 8000+ citations. The authors of the second quote (Egli and Soyka) have credentials that are just as impressive.

Statement:

> *"And we need to be very cautious, because a failed treatment will set a person back."*

Response:

This is fear-mongering with no basis in reality. It implies that medication is likely to fail, with severely negative consequences. But the other available treatments fail consistently—over 90% of the time in fact. So if people are being 'set back' by treatment failure, it is happening every day, with every other treatment anyways. And alcoholism is a chronic, medical condition, of which relapse is a symptom. So there will be setbacks for some people with every treatment.

Why does medication deserve more caution? Does anyone say you should be 'very cautious' about going to AA?

Well, actually some do—and justifiably so—search online for the phrases 'thirteenth step AA' or 'predators in AA' if you'd like more information on the problems vulnerable newcomers and women have experienced in 12-step programs.

Statement:

"Hazelden will never turn its back on pharmaceutical solutions, but..."

Response:

This is like when a person says, "I don't mean to offend, but," then insults you anyways.

One recovering lawyer quoted in an article on addiction commented on this kind of response from places like Hazelden saying:

> *"It's a paradox that some of addicts' biggest advocates have been the most resistant to new treatments...But a lot of them come to the field after recovering from their own addictions, and they can be very stubborn about what works and what doesn't."*[21]

More pointedly, she adds, "some people feel recovery from addiction should *not* be easy or convenient."[21]

So... be ready for the inevitable naysayers you will meet.

And keep in mind–they just don't know any better.

WHEN IS A MEDICATION 'A CRUTCH'?

"The ideal, of course, is to be physically and emotionally healthy
without medications. Just turns out that hasn't been the case for me.
I kinda see the medications as a crutch. But when you're disabled–
either temporarily or permanently–you need a crutch.
And oh, how I can run when I have my crutch!!!"
–Recovering Alcoholic

People who have been involved in 12-step programs often struggle with the idea of incorporating other treatment approaches–instead of or in addition to AA–into their lifestyles. From time to time I have heard people who are influenced by AA, guiltily describing taking medications for alcohol dependence as a 'crutch.'

Sadly, while this belief is outdated and irrational, it's still widely taught and believed in 12-step groups.

When the 12-step based Hazelton treatment center started including medication as a treatment for addiction they had enormous resistance from program members.

Medical Director Marvin Seppala describes the way pressure is sometimes applied to members who choose to take medications:

> "We have had resistance within the 12-step communities. No 12-step groups have resisted specifically what we are talking about or even spoke against it in any public forum.
>
> In keeping with their traditions that hasn't happened.

Individuals, however, certainly have come forward and said things like, "You're ruining AA" and "We don't want your patients on medicine in our meetings."

They refuse to sponsor people on those medications. It's been troublesome from that perspective ... we've actually developed an approach called Stigma Management for our patients. If they're placed on medication and they're attending 12-step meetings, we help them find meetings that are amendable to these medications...

Some people at some meetings won't let people talk about this. They'll really give them a hard time and tell them to get off the medications even though a doctor at one of our facilities has prescribed them."[24]

In Gabrielle Glaser's excellent article, 'The Irrationality of AA', she writes:

"It's not that AA started out as irrational, but when you stand still and do not evolve, while the world evolves and changes around you and you don't question yourself, you can become irrational in comparison."

The crutch concept started out rationally.

There was not a single effective medication for any mental illness in the 1930s when AA was started.

Back then, the lobotomy was still considered cutting-edge and treatment for mental illness was more like torture.

The very first medication for alcoholism was opium. And later, the Keeley Cure helped civil war surgeon Leslie Keeley grow rich by selling a 'scientific' treatment—containing 28% alcohol.

The Keeley Institute treated alcoholics with the 'cure' up until 1939, incidentally the same year the big book of AA was first published.

Other medicinal 'cures' followed—many of them useless, harmful, addictive or all of the above.

So in 1939, and for decades after that, when mental illness was untreatable and alcoholism medication was ineffective at best and addictive at worst, it made a lot of sense to dissuade AA members from relying on any substance or treatment other than AA.

In addition, alcoholism is such an insidious disease—hijacking ones' own thought processes and decision-making—so much so that susceptibility to other addictive substances is something alcoholics must be vigilant about.

In the early thirties, forties and fifties, when there were no good medication options for any kind of mental illness, let alone alcoholism, drawing a line in the sand and saying 'medication is a crutch' was simply a way to help alcoholics steer clear of pitfalls.

There's an analogy that I believe fits AA in many aspects of its existence.

It's a story about a lady who used to cut the top inch off of every turkey she cooked before it went in the oven. When asked why, she said she didn't know why it was done, but it was the way her mother had taught her.

One day, she asked her mother why she used this approach, and her mother responded, "my oven was always too small to fit the bird in it—so I cut a piece off the top."

It's easy to understand AA's original intention and approach, but once again, like many of AA's notions, the idea that medications are unequivocally unacceptable is now doing more harm than good.

If you are someone who is strongly influenced by 12-step principles, and the 'medication is a crutch' issue is problematic for you, then it's time for you to stop cutting the top off the turkey.

And maybe it's time to look at AA as the crutch instead.

Perhaps there is a place for an updated AA program in the future–alcoholics still need a great deal of support–something AA provides well.

But anyone dissuading an alcoholic from taking medication in this century–anyone who thinks they know better than the thousands of gifted medical researchers and addiction specialists whose research is cited in this book series–should consider that they may be helping to sign that alcoholic's death certificate.

Avoid MOM

Medication Option Myopia–MOM for short–is a common downfall that you need to avoid in this process. This book–which presents not just one, but many medication solutions–is attempting to counter this pitfall.

There is a curious phenomenon that affects how we make choices and how we recommend options to others. I'm calling it 'option myopia' for lack of a better term.

When I read Claudia Christian's book about her experiences with alcoholism and finding naltrexone and then watched her documentary, 'One Little Pill,' I became convinced that her direction was the 'right' direction. I disregarded information about other medication I came across.

Later, when I read Dr. Ameisen's book about his experiences and how baclofen (and only baclofen) worked for him, I could see that he was very focused on helping others to access baclofen–and only baclofen. In fact, in some of his writing, I'm sad to say that he criticized those prescribing any medication other than baclofen.

I think it works like this… we think that 'what saved me' is most likely to save you too. And the bigger the impact that solution had on our own lives, the more 'stuck' we become on the idea that it is the ONLY way for anyone else.

And, if you are on the receiving end of advice from someone who is truly passionate and honest about their experience, the more likely we may be to feel that 'what saved them' will 'save me too.'

Option Myopia applies to doctors too (and maybe this is one reason why they aren't prescribing these medications).

But you can see it everywhere–it may be why you want your son to be a lawyer just like you; or why my friend wants me to buy the same kind of car she drives; or why your daughter wants you to be vegan and gluten-free just like her. It's one of the reasons that AA members are also so adamant about AA.

While Option Myopia comes from a good place, it can be very dangerous. You may find it affects you in these ways:

- You will be less likely to get support from others who are emotionally invested in an alternative recovery solution.

- You may become quite emotionally invested in one solution; and if that solution doesn't work for you, may be devastated by the outcome and hesitant to try anything else.

I am here (admittedly with my own biases and myopia) to suggest that you do not pin your hope on one medication: avoid MOM and be completely option neutral.

Come on this journey with the long-term view–that if the first medication doesn't work, there are at least 10 more to try.

And maybe you'll have to try ten before you hit on what works for you. Think of this as a marathon, not a sprint. Do not become emotionally invested in one medication or solution. Be like the scientists–test it, and if it doesn't work, learn and move on.

Recognize it's okay if you don't get support from people who are option myopic themselves–this is inevitable; ignore them.

Remember it is a very few lucky ones who hit on the right medication first–Ameisen, for example, tried AA, short-term rehab, long-term rehab, psychological counseling, disulfiram, naltrexone, acamprosate and topiramate with very little effect before finding that high-dose baclofen worked for him.

And in the end, it was a combination of three solutions that helped Ameisen the most. What brought Ameisen serenity was to apply what he had learned in AA and psychological counseling to a new life with baclofen.

What if you try numerous medications and nothing works?

Then take a break for a few years. And then, one day try again: things are now changing more quickly in this space than they have for decades—so if the current solutions don't work for you, take a break but don't give up.

By the way, don't get option myopic about the broader idea of medication for alcohol treatment either.

Perhaps mindfulness and meditation or some other approach will work for you more effectively. That's perfectly okay.

WHEN TO START

Why *would* you wait?

Should medication be the last resort for someone who has tried every other way to reduce or quit drinking?

Hell no. The earlier, the better.

There is no evidence that medication should be the treatment of last resort, and in fact, given that alcoholism is a disease that becomes progressively more severe and the alcoholic loses more and more control as the disease progresses, it is logical that medication should be one of the first solutions examined.

Doctors do not wait to prescribe effective medications to people who are diagnosed with other serious illnesses (including mental illnesses) until every other possible means of 'natural' or 'spiritual' alternative is extinguished.

Many individuals who are first diagnosed with mental illness not only are often prescribed medication in the very same appointment, but are told that if they *don't* take the medication that other treatment will not be made available to them.

So, particularly given the fact that many of them are very safe, commonly used medications for other illnesses, why should doctors wait to treat alcohol dependence with medication?

It's well documented that progressive alcoholism causes physiological and brain damage ('neuroadaptations') to sufferers. There is no reason to let this damage progress.

Waiting not only weakens one's ability over time to gain control over dependence, but the risk of illness and death increases significantly with every year–so it makes sense that alcohol dependence is treated–right from its identification–in a much more aggressive way perhaps even than other mental illnesses.

The medication may have more of a fighting chance in someone with a weaker addiction, and whose body and mind are still in some ways healthy (versus many years down the road when other medications and illnesses could further hamper recovery), and who still have social supports, such as friends and family and employment, in place.

BRING YOUR GRAIN OF SALT

One of the themes of this book is educating yourself.

But as you are reading through research, or hearing the comments of others about personal or scientific findings (whether it's online or in a doctor's office) I recommend taking their conclusions with a grain of salt.

With so little knowledge and clear information available about treatments for alcoholism, mistruths are rife.

In one forum I remember reading a posting about one medication that said, "scientists thought that XYZ was true, but that was completely disproven in a recent study."

You can't draw a conclusion from a single study–unlike the poster stated, a single study cannot completely prove or disprove anything.

Conclusions can only be drawn with some degree of accuracy after multiple well-run studies have been conducted properly by different scientists, that reproduce the finding of the first study. So I caution you never to base your conclusions on one study or one comment.

Even in scientific research, it seems that sometimes there is an agenda behind certain conclusions. (And that is just one reason why a high-quality *body* of research–not just one or two studies–is important to take into consideration).

For example, one of the things that have surprised me as I read through all of the research I have is how easy it is to 'prove' that something doesn't work if you really want to.

Some of the research I have read almost seems like it is setting a medication up for failure on purpose. (In these cases I wonder what political or financial gain is behind the design of the test.)

For example, one piece of research that caught my eye is an article called, "Comparison of baclofen vs. naltrexone treatment during abstinence on the reinstatement of alcohol self-administration in baboons"[25] which was published in the *Journal of Drug and Alcohol Dependence* in 2015.

The first part of all research reports contain an abstract, which is a summary of the experiment, its results, and conclusions. The stark results of this piece of research were stated at the end of the abstract:

"Conclusions: These data do not support the use of baclofen during early abstinence to reduce relapse to heavy drinking."

It's so easy to scan this research and conclude simply that 'baclofen doesn't work,' from this statement.

However, the way that baclofen was administered to baboons in this experiment is completely different to the way researchers have found baclofen must be administered to humans in order to be effective.

Specifically, baboons were given small doses of baclofen beginning on day 1 of a 5-day forced abstinence period and it was found that they drank just as much on day 6 as baboons taking another alcohol dependence drug—naltrexone (which is known to decrease drinking).

However, baclofen has been shown to work best under completely different circumstances.

It's recommended to slowly taper up dosage over the course of weeks or months, maintain a very high maximum dose (a much higher maximum amount than the grams per kg tested with the baboons), for a month or more until a switch point where reduced craving and desire for alcohol is achieved, and then slowly taper down to a maintenance level.

That's an entirely different scenario than those poor drunken baboons experienced.

The conclusion for the baboon test should perhaps instead have been this instead:

"When administered in a way that has never been shown to work, and we didn't really think would work, baclofen does not work."

STEP 2: DESIGN YOUR PATHWAY

WHICH DRUG WORKS BEST?

After facing a barren landscape of non-medical treatment options for alcoholism for years, you may now find yourself overwhelmed by the plethora of pharmaceuticals that actually are realistic options for you.

So, the question is, which one do you start with?

If I (or anyone) could tell you which drug will work best for you, they would be sitting on their own private island drinking beer out of a golden stein right now.

I promise you that the best that science has to offer is at most a pretty uneducated guess about which medications you should try first, and second and third…

If someone is 'certain' about anything related to these drugs (certain they will work, or certain they won't work, or certain about the 'best' one), then I can tell you with 100% confidence that person is not someone whose advice you should hold in high regard.

That is because the *only* certainty in this field right now, today, is that nobody can tell you that.

We just do not know enough about alcoholism and how each drug works to predict which drug will work for which person. At this time, it is impossible to rule out a drug (due to lack of predicted effectiveness) in anybody.

The only way to know for sure if a medication will help you is to try it.

And that is why, when deciding which drugs to try first, I recommend you think about your plan as a 'Medication Pathway.'

And by this I mean, instead of selecting *the drug*, create a list of drugs. Ask yourself: Based on what I know about myself and these medications–which might be the first drug I try? And then the second drug? And then the third one, and then the fourth, and so on.

Don't choose a drug–choose a pathway.

•••

Do you remember the game 'Mastermind'?

It's a code breaking game. The code maker hides a set of four colored pegs at the end of a plastic board. The codebreaker tries different combinations of pegs, one set of four at a time. After each attempt, the code maker gives hints about the accuracy of the guess. The code breaker gets 12 different tries to get it right, solving the code through trial and error.

Choosing a medication for alcoholism is a lot like a game of Mastermind.

That's not very helpful when it comes to narrowing down where to begin, though.

So here is how you will go about determining which medications you need to try.

CREATE A LONG LIST

To start with, read Book 4 in this series.

- Book 4 covers the characteristics that give hints as to which medications may or may not work. So as you read, write down your personal characteristics–whether you think you are a Type A or B alcoholic or a combination; if you have other health concerns; if you smoke or not; if your alcoholism is what you use to treat another illness like anxiety or depression; write down your goals.

- Then read through the list of medications. As you read, take a few notes about the ones you think might be helpful for you based on your own personal characteristics.

Those notes (and any other information you gather elsewhere) will help you create a 'long list' of drugs.

The A-List and B-Lists contain 15 medications in total. You may be able to cross a few off your list, or lower their priority just through what you learn about yourself and the medications.

Research has given us 'directional clues' about medication.

For example, research has shown that some medications work better for Type B than Type A alcoholism, and other medications seem to work better for those motivated to drink by reward (versus motivated by anxiety). (Type and drinking motivation are discussed in more detail later).

These directional clues can help you choose where to start or what to try next.

But keep in mind that for every little clue we have that suggests a drug *may not* work for someone, there are examples where that drug worked very well for that person.

And for every clue we have that a particular drug *will* and *should* work for someone, there are examples of people it has been completely ineffective in.

And as frustrating and as hit-or-miss as this may be, the fact that you can't rule too many drugs out because there's little proof it *won't* work is, at least, a hopeful thing. (It means it's very difficult to run out of options).

This hit-or-miss approach is the one recommended by scientists.

Raye Z. Litten, Ph.D. Associate Director Division of Treatment and Recovery Research National Institute on Alcohol Abuse and Alcoholism (NIAAA) says, "what we hope to do is to actually have a menu of treatments that clinicians could choose from. If one drug doesn't work or they can't tolerate it," patients would "try another one and so forth, and hopefully they'll find one that is effective."[3]

If that process leaves you confused, know that any one of the medications on the A-List has a wealth of data supporting its effectiveness, so starting with one or two drugs on that list may be as good a start as any.

You could simply do this–start with the first medication on the A-List and begin with that one, and work your way down.

NARROW TO A SHORT LIST

Next, your long list can be made into a shorter list due to other factors.

These factors are less to do with effectiveness and more to do with aspects like availability, commitment and safety, than effectiveness.

For example, when choosing a medication to start with, ask yourself these questions:

Availability:

- Is it available in my country?

- Will my doctor prescribe it?

- Can I afford it?

Commitment:

- Are the potential side effects tolerable? Am I willing to take the medication even if they make me feel sick, spacey or tired?

- If availability will be a barrier, am I willing to pursue other ways of obtaining it?

Safety:

- Will it interact with other medications I take?

- Can I take it despite existing health concerns?

LEARN FROM YOUR EXPERIENCES

Once you begin to try a medication, pay very close attention to your behaviors, thoughts and actions. Identify any variations you can. These will be clues in your journey.

For example–let's say you feel a strong effect from naltrexone. Maybe the first few times you try it, instead of drinking that whole bottle of wine, you just walk away from it.

Later you drink on it but you don't feel what you are looking for from the alcohol.

A few days later, you avoid taking the pill before you drink and you give up on naltrexone.

Great! That's not a failure.

You've learned four valuable things:

1) Your brain responds to naltrexone.

2) Naltrexone removes some pleasure from your drinking.

3) Your alcoholism may be tied to the reward system in the brain (the part that includes dopamine and the opioid system which makes drinking feel good).

4) You have trouble with 'as needed' medication.

What can you do with that information?

You can:

- Try another naltrexone method (such as monthly injection).

- Try another medication that works differently but targets the reward system–such as topiramate.

- Add another medication that helps you with that impulsiveness that leads you to jump straight to the drink without the pill. Like acamprosate or even disulfiram.

- Try some combination of the above options.

Learning these things and applying them to the process is exactly what will move you down that game board toward success.

And as you eliminate medications by trying them, use what you have learned to revise that pathway. One day you may land upon the perfect combination for you.

Mastermind!

WHAT TYPE ARE YOU?

One of the most important clues you can use to determine which medications to take is the type of alcoholic you are. Read on to learn more about determining whether you are Type A, or Type B.

But first, imagine this scenario:

There may be 10 people in a room, all of whom drink excessively, none of whom have the ability to control their alcohol intake, and whose drinking is damaging to themselves and to those around them.

All ten might be considered to have 'textbook alcoholism'. All ten would receive the same diagnosis.[26]

But do all ten have the same disease?

Probably not.

They each may have very different sets of genes and environmental variables that put them at risk. And these very different genes may contribute to very different imbalances in their brains and bodies that all ultimately result in alcohol addiction.

Understanding this is the key to understanding why one medication for alcoholism will work extremely well in one alcoholic, and have no effect whatsoever in another.

There is more and more evidence that there are at least two types of alcoholism: Type A and Type B.[27] As research progresses, other types will be identified.

Type A and Type B are probably made up of two separate (but sometimes intersecting) pools of very different genetic variations. But because we don't have conclusive genetic testing for alcoholism, the way that we determine Alcoholism Type is based on two factors driven by those genetic variations.

Those two factors are:

1) When your heavy drinking began.

2) Whether you have a family history of alcoholism or not.

As research progresses, types (and their corresponding medical treatments) will probably be at least partially (if not completely) delineated based on findings related to your DNA.

Genetic variations hold the key to whether a medication will work for you or not. And correspondingly, we have been able to see that some gene variations seem to occur more frequently in Type A alcoholics, and other variations appear more frequently in Type B's.

So it may be very useful for you to try to classify yourself–if possible–as one of the two types. You may find that you are the very definition of one of the types, or you may find that you have overlapping characteristics shared by both.

Here is how both are described:

Type B alcoholism ('Early Onset Alcoholism') is described as[27]:

- the most distinct form

- thought to be present in 65% of alcohol-dependent people[28]

- due to its higher severity, this subtype is seen more frequently in treatment or medical facilities

- characterized by an early age of onset (before the age of 25)

- tendency toward high impulsivity

- strong family history of alcoholism

- motivated early on by strong enjoyment of drinking

Type A alcoholism ('Late Onset Alcoholism') is described as[27]:

- everyone else

- thought to be present 35% of alcohol-dependent subjects[28]

- anxious personality traits may be a characteristic feature

If you are struggling to determine which type you may be, researcher Bankole Johnson suggests that the best way to determine whether you are a type A or B alcoholic is to ask a single question: "…at what age did drinking become a problem for you?"[27]

If it became a problem early–before the age of 25, then you may be Type B; if it was later–after the age of 25, then you may be a Type A.

If you find it hard to remember which type is which, this trick might help: The word 'late' has a distinctive 'A' sound in it. Remember the word 'lAte' associated with type A alcoholism and you won't get confused.

And the phrase 'the early bird gets the worm' can help too, since 'bird' starts with a 'B', and Type Bs start early.

RELATIONSHIP BETWEEN TYPES & MEDS

It is thought that in Type B alcoholics, early alcohol consumption is driven by a strong biological need for positive reinforcement of the brain's reward system.

In other words, Type B alcoholics may crave from an early age the feelings and experiences that alcohol brings.

In contrast, Type A alcoholics' consumption may be driven by an entirely different process—for example, an imbalance in the stress hormone system which generates feelings that the individual seeks to numb and lessen with alcohol.

In short, it's hypothesized that in general, Type B's are driven by pleasure (and alcoholism may be more reinforced by malfunctions in the reward centres of the brain), and Type A's are driven to numb pain (and perhaps related more to stress systems).

It's this thinking that reveals why medicines work for different types. Pleasure/reward and pain/stress are generated and controlled by very different brain systems. And different medications are used to target these different brain systems.

Earlier in the book I mentioned how knowing the type of alcoholism you may have can help you narrow down the medications to try.

As you read through descriptions of medications and research highlights in the next book you'll come across examples where research into specific medications showed different results for Type A alcoholics than Type B alcoholics.

Ondansetron is an example of one of the medications where this has been found to be the case. Researcher Dr. Bankole Johnson showed that ondansetron reduced drinking in Type B alcoholics, but was ineffective in Type A patients.

Johnson hypothesized that this is because ondansetron impacts receptors in the brain that interfere with the positive reinforcement the brain provides when alcohol is present. In other words–it interferes with the pleasure that Type B's seek. And over time it may weaken the brain's conditioning, decreasing craving and drive for alcohol.

Bankole was also able to connect the success of ondansetron specifically to a group of Type B alcoholics with specific genetic variations. He found that alcoholics carrying a combination of the same five gene variations were able to reduce their drinking when taking ondansetron.

One of the combinations within these 5 gene variations were held by individuals who responded in such a positive way to ondansetron that he termed this group 'super-responders'.[29]

And notably, for alcoholics in the study *without* these genetic markers, being treated with ondansetron actually worsened their alcohol consumption.

Johnson suggests that a DNA test that looks for these five genetic markers will one day predict the outcome of treatment by ondansetron in alcoholics.

He is not the only researcher who thinks DNA testing will help alcoholics find the best treatment. The Director of the National Institute on Alcohol Abuse and Alcoholism (NIAAA), Dr. George Koob says, "Our hope is that down the line, we might be able to do a simple blood test that tells if you will be a naltrexone person, an acamprosate person, a ghrelin person.[30]

Better yet, perhaps eventually, we'll use this testing to prevent alcoholism in the first place.

As researcher Dr. Marc A Schuckit says, "it's theoretically possible to take kids before they first drink, find out whether they have any gene variations, and say to them, 'If you choose to be a drinker, then be careful."[3]

IMPORTANT DISCOVERY: DNA TESTING

At the time I wrote the first book, I was unaware of how DNA-testing services like 23andme.com worked, and I reported that there was no private DNA-testing company that had a specific test for alcoholism. (And as far as I know, that's still the case).

However, recently, 23andme.com became available where I live and for under $300 I was able to get my own DNA tested and learned how the service worked. This was both a very eye-opening experience for me and one which I recommend that anyone who is trying to narrow down medications to treat drinking pursue.

This service (and others similar to it) takes your saliva sample, scans it for hundreds of genetic variations that the research community is studying, and provides you with all of the data on your own genetic variations. The service doesn't provide data on every single one of your genetic variations – just a subset of the ones they've deemed most important for a variety of health conditions and traits.

Then, you can use another tool (I used promethease.com–a tool I highly recommend–for $5) to analyze and delve into what the data that 23andme.com has provided to you means.

One of the things that I did with promethease was to search my genetic data for the five gene variations that Dr. Bankole reported would be indicative of my response to the drug ondansetron.

Of the five variations, 23andme.com provided me with data on four of them (perhaps in the future the fifth variation will also be reported by this service).

I was able to see from this data that I did not carry any of the genetic variations that Johnson's research has indicated show that ondansetron would be effective for me if I were to take it for alcoholism.

What this tells me is that if I were an alcoholic, I might not begin with ondansetron—in fact, I would probably stay away from it.

However, if I were a carrier of the variations that Johnson had identified as significant, 23andme.com would show me at least four out of five of them, and I might be very interested in taking ondansetron as one of the first drugs I tried.

The discovery that for under $300 I could help refine my medication pathway (potentially allowing me to find the medication that works for me much sooner) is an enormous one. My only regret is that my friend Randy passed away before I discovered this.

Johnson's work is not the only work that is connecting the dots between alcoholism, genes, and medications.

At least six of the medications discussed in this book respond to alcoholism in individuals with specific genetic variants.

For example, topiramate has been shown to work more effectively on carriers of a variation of the GRIK1 gene.

Naltrexone's efficacy seems tied to variations of OPRM1 and DRD4; sertraline shows promise in carriers of variations of 5HTTLPR[31]; and people with a variation of the gene GATA4 have shown improvement with acamprosate.[32]

For doxazosin, scientists that saw that alcoholics with a strong family history saw a drinking reduction, but for those with little family history of alcoholism, increased drinking was seen.[33]

OFF-LABEL MEDICATIONS

"My doctor won't prescribe it to me because it is off label, and he says he could lose his license."

Understanding what 'off-label' means and what its implications are, is critical to being able to advocate for yourself with your doctor.

This is because the statement above, written by someone in an online forum who was seeking a prescription for topiramate for the treatment of their alcoholism, represents a common, but false misconception. Doctors often prescribe medications that are off-label, and in many cases, would not be acting in the patient's best interest if they didn't prescribe off-label medications.

Let's step back and look at the approval process and what prescribing on- and off-label really means.

The term 'FDA-Approved', means a medication has been approved by the United States Food and Drug Administration.

If you are in Canada, the equivalent term is that a drug has been 'Approved by Health Canada'.

In Europe, the drug has been 'Approved by the European Medicines Agency (EMA)'.

All three of these organizations are responsible for evaluating and regulating medicinal products within their regions.

A drug company interested in selling a prescription drug must test it in various ways. First are lab and animal experiments and next are human tests to see if the drug is safe and effective in humans.

After testing, the drug company sends the FDA an application with the test results and a proposed label. The label indicates the illnesses it has been shown effective for, possible risks, and the approved dosage.

For example, many years ago, a drug called Quinine was FDA-Approved as an anti-malaria medication. This means it went through testing and was shown safe and effective specifically for this purpose. So, when prescribed in the FDA-approved manner, it is prescribed only as protection against malaria—as per the label instruction.

Quinine is now far more likely to be prescribed by doctors for people who suffer from nighttime leg cramps than as protection against malaria. It is often prescribed as a first line treatment for leg cramps (meaning it may be one of the first options a doctor suggests you try).

When it is prescribed for leg cramps, it is prescribed 'off-label.'

If it were prescribed for anti-malaria purposes, but at *double* the FDA-approved dosage, it would also be called an 'off-label' prescription.

Drug companies often learn about other uses for their medications before submitting the FDA application but choose not to seek regulatory approval for the other use.

The entire process of testing and application development is very expensive, so whether the drug company decides to submit another application for the other use or not is based solely on a cost-benefit analysis.

The effectiveness of a medication, and its on- or off-label status are much less related than you might assume.

It is important to know that a medication is not 'off-label' because it is not proven or effective. 'Off-label' and effectiveness are completely unrelated.

A drug can be extremely safe and effective and be better than on-label treatments yet be off-label for the treatment of alcoholism *simply* because it has not been in a drug company's best financial interests to apply for approval for the specific purpose of treatment of alcohol use disorders. Drug development and approval is motivated solely by shareholder value–not altruism.

The three drugs that have had on-label approval for alcoholism in North America are the same three mentioned earlier as being 'first line': acamprosate, naltrexone, and disulfiram.

It is illegal for pharmaceutical companies to market drugs for their known off-label purposes.

So, for example, even though Quinine can be legally prescribed by doctors as a medication that helps nighttime leg cramps, drug companies are not allowed to promote or market or even speak to doctors about Quinine's use for leg cramps.

Quinine could have a thousand research studies supporting its incredible leg cramp capability but without going through an approval process and gaining FDA-approval, the drug company that owns it can never–will never–say a word to a doctor about it.

Whether or not to prescribe medication for an on-label or off-label purpose is solely the decision of the doctor. It is an entirely legal and very common practice.

Prescribing off-label can be very beneficial to patients (for example–those suffering nighttime leg cramps), but doctors can be averse to doing so because it also has its risks.

Doctors don't want to open themselves up to the risk that patients under their care will be harmed by a drug that has not been tested for the purpose for which the drug is being prescribed.[34]

For example, Quinine was never officially tested for the purpose for which it is used most.

And incidentally, in 2011, Health Canada issued an advisory that it had received 71 reports of serious adverse reactions to Quinine, 67 of which were for prescriptions for leg cramps, not malaria.

But despite doctor's fears, off-label prescribing happens every day, is completely within the doctor's legal rights to do, and is necessary to patient care.

The American Medical Association says that the deciding factor in off-label prescribing is up to the doctor and based on "the best interest of the patient."[35]

The FDA only regulates drug approval–not drug prescribing. According to one expert, doctors are:

> *"Free to prescribe a drug for any reason they think is medically appropriate and off-label use is so common that virtually every drug is used off-label in some circumstances."*[36]

Off-label prescribing is extremely common. Over 23 percent (more than one in five) of all prescriptions and over 60 percent in cancer care are off-label.[35]

In Canada, nearly 80% of prescriptions for rare diseases are off-label.[37]

And in fact, regarding doctor's prescribing habits, and the ethics around them, so few medicines are approved for rare diseases that doctors would be acting *unethically* if they only prescribed on-label medications for rare illnesses.

Alcoholism is the same in this regard–with so few approved medications for its treatment–it could be argued that any doctor refusing to prescribe off-label medication for its treatment is also acting unethically.

There is one other thing that is important to know about off-label prescribing and it relates to drug coverage.

Medications that are prescribed for off-label treatments can fall into a loophole in many insurance coverage plans. Some plans may restrict reimbursement to medications prescribed for on-label purposes only.

Of course, this can create burdensome cost implications for anyone seeking treatment for alcohol use disorders and can (and probably will) severely limit the medications you may be able to get coverage for.

So knowing in advance whether your coverage plan will cover an off-label use for medication you are requesting from your doctor can impact the way you may choose to go about selecting and obtaining medication.

But the bottom line is that if a doctor is telling you that they can lose their license for prescribing one of the drugs in this book to you (particularly if it is one of the ones in the heavily-researched A-List), then it may be time to try to educate the old one, or look for a new one.

ARE THESE DRUGS ADDICTIVE?

Of all of the medications found in Book 4, there are only two which raise any kind of concerns in regard to addictive qualities.

The first is Sodium Oxybate, which is found very last on the B-List.

I wasn't sure whether to include it on the B-List or not because of its addictive nature, and that is why it is last on the list.

Finally, I included it because, despite its addictive qualities: (a) there is a great deal of research showing its exceptional effectiveness; (b) a new formulation is being developed which will include deterrents to its use in addictive behavior; and (c) it has been used for many years successfully as a treatment in Italy for alcoholism.

I think that, should the new formulation (with addiction-deterrents) be successful, then Sodium Oxybate could one day find itself on the A-List.

The second is gabapentin, which is found on the A-List.

This drug is not addictive by itself. It is also a common medication prescribed in high volumes by many physicians around the world.

However, it has been found to be used as a booster (a drug that makes another drug more potent) for other addictive behavior in a very small number of cases.

If your addiction is limited to alcohol, and you do not abuse any other substance, then you need not have any concerns about gabapentin in regard to addiction.

COMBINING MEDICATIONS

Adjunctive therapy is the term used to describe adding a second medication or other treatment to make a first one more effective.

For example, adjunctive therapy might include adding acamprosate to your naltrexone regime, or it could mean adding cognitive behavioral therapy to your naltrexone regime.

For the treatment of alcoholism, adjunctive therapy–with a second or even a third medication–has a higher probability of working for you than treatment with only one medication. (Though because so many alcoholics have trouble even getting the first prescription for even one medication, it's only a lucky few who are able to access this kind of multi-drug treatment).

There is good reason for this approach and it is one that holds greater promise as more research is done.[27]

First, more than one neurotransmitter system in the brain is affected by alcoholism and different medications target different systems, which target different feelings and behaviors found in alcoholism.

So one medication can be working on one system while another medication is working on another.

Second, multiple medications can target other psychiatric conditions that often come hand-in-hand with alcoholism–from depression to anxiety to bipolar or schizophrenia.

Third, a lower dose of each of two drugs can minimize the side effects experienced with a higher dose of a single drug; and this, in turn, can improve adherence to the treatment.

Fourth, by combining medications, synergistic effects can be found–the drugs can build on each other resulting in a better end-result for the patient compared to improvements of each drug individually.

And finally, choosing a medication is very hit or miss–a medication often will work for only one out of five to ten individuals (similar to anti-depressants), so it increases your odds of finding a solution sooner if you are able to try more than one at a time, especially when the ones you are trying are acting on different systems in the brain.

A recent study by respected NIAAA researcher Dr. Lorenzo Leggio looked at seventeen different clinical studies (eleven of which were high quality, randomized, double-blind and placebo controlled) that investigated combinations of medications in alcoholism.

It found that ten of the eleven high-quality studies showed the combination of drugs to be superior to placebo and that three out of eleven showed an overall advantage of the combination.[38]

While several of the drugs in this book have been combined in some research and shown promising results, there is still little research on the combining of medications to treat alcoholism. (There is a shortage of funding for research and development in alcohol addiction as it is, and so research that looks at multiple medications at once is lacking).

However, for individuals who are pursuing their own treatment, looking at medication combinations could be very promising.

So as you consider your medication options, ask yourself whether combinations may be worth looking into.

You may wish to consider a multi-medication strategy.

MULTI-MEDICATION STRATEGY EXAMPLE

A multi-medication strategy could be used to break down the elements of alcoholism you struggle with and target them separately.

For example, you may want to look at one drug as a way to weaken your cravings and decrease responsiveness to stress or alcohol cues; while another medication could be selected based on your experience when drinking on it (lessening the pleasure of drinking or increasing your ability to stop after fewer drinks).

So for example, if you are trying to remain abstinent perhaps a combination of acamprosate and naltrexone could be considered.

The acamprosate may help you manage cravings which could lead to relapse; and the naltrexone may lessen the reward of drinking so that you drink less if you do lapse.

And if you do relapse, while this book does not cover medications that help with alcohol withdrawal, several medications can make withdrawal, and the process of getting back on your feet again afterward, less physically and mentally defeating.

For example, two in this book: baclofen and gabapentin, have been shown to help with withdrawal severity.

So a plan which attacks your alcoholism with a three-pronged approach might work for you: One to deter you from relapse for as long as possible; one to minimize the extent of the lapse itself;

and a third to help you recover from the lapse as quickly as possible, to regain your equilibrium and health quickly.

While this may not be a 'cure' for your alcoholism, the severity and impact on your life could be greatly minimized by an approach such as this.

I'm not suggesting that you start dosing yourself with massive quantities of every kind of pill you can obtain.

The point I'm trying to make here is to be strategic.

If you can stand back and with your doctor's help assess the areas where you need the greatest support, then it's possible you could put a combination of medications in place that allow you to manage your alcoholism. Other chronic diseases are managed in the same way–with multiple medications that target different elements of the disease, allowing life to be livable.

Instead of having it continue to destroy you, it's possible that you might be able to use medications and other tools available to minimize alcoholism's impact on your life and health.

When considering combinations, always look at the available research on combinations (see the Q&A section for each medication for combinations that have been researched together), and always check for drug interactions.

This can be done at online medication checkers, with your doctor or your pharmacist.

OTHER CONSIDERATIONS

There are many considerations you may wish to take into account when determining which medication to try (or to try next).

AVAILABILITY

What you can Obtain–At the Correct Dosage

Your doctor may not wish to prescribe medication to you at the doses that have been shown to be effective by research.

For example, research has shown that baclofen at very high doses (even as high as 300mg per day or more) may be required for effectiveness for some individuals. Sadly, many doctors are only comfortable prescribing up to 30mg of Baclofen per day for alcoholism.

If this is the most you are able to have prescribed to you, then it might be better to try another option instead.

Or, some individuals have reported that they will accept the prescription from their doctor anyways and then looked for other avenues where the dosage amount can be topped up–such as purchasing from an online pharmacy. In this way, some people are still able to have a doctor medically overlook their treatment, though they are actually dosing themselves at higher amounts. (As mentioned earlier–I don't recommend this–taking greater doses of medication without your doctor's knowledge can be extremely dangerous. However I also recognize the extreme treatment gap many patients face.)

If you have already tried one or more of the medications in this book and found them ineffective, it may be worthwhile for you to revisit just *how* they were prescribed to you. It is *very* possible, (especially if you tried baclofen), that you were not prescribed an effective dose.

Don't rely solely on a single doctor's knowledge about dosage or what will or will not work. Learn as much as you can from research and online from others so that *you* can determine the approach you want to take–and then work hard to get that plan implemented *with* your doctor.

What's approved in Your Country or One you can Visit

Not all medications are available in all countries. Earlier I wrote about ways that some people have gotten around this–for example, by going to another country or ordering online.

If ordering online or leaving the country for treatment are not steps you wish to take then you may need to cross some medications off of your long list.

For anyone in Canada, naltrexone injection will need to be crossed off the list.

And unless you are in a country like Italy, where Sodium Oxybate has more acceptance and traction, Sodium Oxybate will probably be one to cross off too.

And because a version of Sodium Oxybate is illicit (GHB), don't even consider trying to buy it online or taking it over a border.

If you'd like to try nalmefene, you may only be able to get it in Europe at the moment, so naltrexone may be a close alternative to try.

Cost and Health Plan Coverage

There are some ways that may make medication less expensive for you. Here are a few:

- Lower costs by asking for generic drugs where they are available or by buying outside your area or over the internet if you can find a good quality source. Medications have very different price tags in different countries and in states and provinces within those countries.

- Look for ways to apply discounts (for example on the Vivitrol website–naltrexone injection–there is an opportunity to apply for an immediate $500 discount on the cost of the injection).

- Ask your doctor for free samples of prescribed drugs to help cover costs. (In Europe, samples for nalmefene, which is currently being marketed by Lundbeck to doctors there may be available to physicians who ask).

- Investigate insurance options which might cover certain medications. In Canada for example, there is an extensive list of medications not typically automatically covered, but for which you can apply to the government for coverage. You may need to dig a little to find out these types of options no matter where you live.

- Consider not just the per-pill cost of medication, but the cost of the medication at full dose for an extended period of time to be effective. (But if this seems exorbitant, don't forget to consider the cost to you and your family of your drinking and alcoholism over time too—as it may be far more 'expensive').

- Because of healthcare reforms and the 2008 mental health parity law, plans that did not cover you a few years ago may cover you now. The law that was put in place was intended to end discrimination in health insurance coverage seen in coverage of mental illness. Coverage providers may not be aware that alcohol dependence is a mental illness and should be covered by insurance just as treatment for any other mental illness would be.

SAFETY

Currently Drinking or Abstinent

Most of the medications on the A- and B-Lists (while not necessarily recommended) can be initiated and taken safely during detox and even while drinking.

The only significant exception to this is disulfiram—which is designed to cause major physical discomfort if it is in your system at the same time as alcohol. Never drink with disulfiram in your system.

There are two medications—naltrexone and nalmefene—that doctors are now being encouraged to prescribe in an 'as needed' manner. This means that they would be taken an hour before drinking. So if you are abstinent and wish to stay that way, the 'as needed' approach would not be for you.

However, research has also shown that for some people both of those medications can be taken (and may be helpful) even if you are abstinent and wish to remain so.

Side Effects

You may experience intolerable side effects with the same medication that others experience no side effects for. If you do experience side effects, under the care of a physician, here are a few things you can do:

- Slowly taper down your dose until you reach a dose that is more tolerable, and then very slowly and gradually increase the dosage until you get to the desired dose again. Sometimes your body needs more time to adjust.

- If you must stay at a lower dose, consider adding a second medication to your approach.

- Look at additional online information for the drug to see whether others experienced the side effects and found a way to minimize or tolerate them (or if they diminished over time).

- Remember—you and your support system are in the driver's seat here—take an active role in investigating and minimizing side effects. Always pay attention to what you are experiencing and then investigate their seriousness.

- These are serious medications that can have some rare, but real side-effects that can harm you. Go to your doctor if you have concerns.

- Be an educated consumer—read everything you can about the medication you are considering taking and be aware of all drug interactions, black label warnings, and side effects before you begin. Be smart and do your research.

- Sometimes there are simple over-the-counter products that can help with side-effects. For example, stomach problems and head-aches can be treated effectively separately. Sleeping pills can be prescribed that will help with insomnia. For loss of appetite, meal-replacement drinks can be helpful temporarily. Anti-nausea medication like gravol, or stronger medication can help with nausea. Problem-solve and try to research and find solutions for the side-effects before choosing to discontinue medication because of the effects.

- As long as you have checked with your doctor and side-effects are not health-threatening in any way, why not hold on for another week?

Existing Health Concerns and Drug Interactions

Alcoholism is confusing and stubborn enough without trying to treat it in tandem with another illness.

However, the fact is that concurrent mental and physical illnesses are extremely common experiences for those with alcoholism. In some cases they probably share some of the same genes.

If you have a concurrent illness, please be particularly careful to check drug interactions, dose up slowly and with caution, observe yourself carefully and ask your support system to give you feedback if they notice unusual emotional or physical changes in you. If you have a concurrent illness, it's even more important that you only take medication under a doctor's care.

Another health concern to be very careful with is liver damage. Alcoholism can seriously strain and damage your liver, so existing liver damage may narrow down your choices of medication too.

Some of the drugs in the book have been found to be quite safe for people with liver conditions, but work with your doctor closely on this. A government database related to drug-induced liver injury can be a helpful resource in this regard and is found at:

livertox.nih.gov

For some individuals, it may be most important to treat a concurrent illness first before trying a medication in this book.

If you are managing multiple illnesses, it's even more important that you find a doctor that can work closely and flexibly with you. If your current doctor is inflexible, then that may be the first issue you need to remedy.

Run any other pharmaceuticals or non-prescribed medications (for example opioids) through an online drug interaction checker to ensure that one medication will not interact with another you are taking.

Or ask a pharmacist to assess the interaction between one drug and another.

Drug interactions can be life threatening–make sure your approach is a safe one.

Safety & Trade-offs

Nobody *wants* to take medication for anything.

And safety concerns are very valid. The medications in this book can harm you if taken the wrong way.

However, if safety is a major barrier for you, consider the alternatives.

Compare the risks of taking these medications with the risk of continuing on the path you are on.

For some people, the path they are on will kill them–sooner rather than later. And for these people, the question I might put to them is: 'what do you really have to lose by trying?'

Maybe it is helpful to put this in a different perspective.

If you were told that radiation and chemotherapy were required to put your cancer in remission, there would be very few people who would opt not to undergo the treatment.

Yet radiation and chemotherapy expose people to both harmful short-term side-effects and enormous, long-term medical risks.

The side-effects and long-term health risks of current alcohol treatment drugs are mild or practically non-existent, in comparison. And these are medications that are fighting a disease that is just as serious as cancer.

If you have severe alcoholism, what choice do you really have?

For me, it's a no-brainer. If I were an alcoholic, I wouldn't hesitate. And if my parent or my child were alcoholic I would encourage them in this direction in a heartbeat. But that's just me.

COMMITMENT

You may be able to walk into their doctor's office with the right materials and approach, and convince them to prescribe either of the two first-line medications, naltrexone or acamprosate.

And if you are lucky, these drugs will be the right ones for you and you can begin to regain control of your life again.

However for others, this process will take a much larger degree of commitment. You will run into some barriers.

You'll need to jump through hoops finding a doctor that will work with you to access medications that are not first line.

They may be expensive; you may have to go to another country to obtain them; after working hard to obtain the medication, it may not be effective for you; you'll try medications where the side effects are uncomfortable.

This process may not be easy. I can practically guarantee you that it will not be easy.

But the only *true* barrier is your commitment to the process.

If you assume now that you will have barriers like these, then when you come to them they will be less difficult to accept. You'll know that all you have to do is keep pushing and looking for alternatives.

You can check every barrier you come to off on the list of 'problems in the system' and then try to work to change them later when you have your life back.

So determine your level of commitment now, and stick to it.

Compliance

'Compliance' sounds like a word used by accountants or interrogators. Or even worse, accountant interrogators. Bad joke.

But in medicine, compliance means you are following the directions that the doctor gave you regarding a prescription.

Some alcoholics are able to take medication, without their brains talking them out of it. Others have more difficulty.

Determining the option that will work best for you requires a certain level of honesty and self-assessment.

There are several medications known to present a challenge to some individuals in the area of compliance. These include disulfiram and naltrexone (and also perhaps nalmefene).

The effect of drinking alcohol while disulfiram is in your system is not one that anyone wishes to experience, not to mention being very dangerous to your health.

So if you simply cannot stay away from drinking, disulfiram may not be a good choice for you as you'll have trouble with compliance on this medication.

Naltrexone (via the Sinclair Method) and nalmefene are taken as needed–this means that you must have the ability to choose to take these drugs an hour before drinking, each and every time you drink. If that is not something you can commit to, then they may not be a good choice.

Baclofen requires several doses at varying times during the day–this not only requires commitment but also a certain level of sobriety to be able to carry through with the correct dosing.

For people where compliance is a serious problem, naltrexone by monthly injection may be a good option because commitment and follow-through only have to happen 12 times a year. (Or twice a year for the 6-month injection version).

You may not realize you have trouble with compliance until you begin taking a medication, and then don't follow through on it.

That's okay. Don't beat yourself up. Learn from it, and move on to an alternative approach.

Step 3: The Bigger Plan

Spokes on a Wheel

You medication plan is part of a bigger plan.

This book focusses on medication. But just like any illness, you need to consider and take into account the balance of your entire lifestyle.

Think of your bigger plan like a wheel–with you in the center surrounded by spokes.

Each spoke represents an important part of your health. For example:

- Getting enough sleep

- Eating a healthy diet

- Connecting with others

- Continuing to gather knowledge

- Dealing with other medical issues

- Gathering support from positive sources

- Medication and treatment plan

- Physical activity

- Minimizing stress

- Dealing with financial issues

- Maintaining mental health

The stronger each of those spokes are, the greater likelihood that you will be okay if one of those spokes breaks down. You'll still be held up by the others.

For example-if you are getting enough sleep, eating well, connecting with others, building your knowledge and addressing all other medical conditions, then if you come across major obstacles in your medication and treatment plan, those obstacles won't affect you as much.

However, if you are overtired, undernourished, lonely, uninformed, and sick, and then run into obstacles, you are going to have a much weaker ability to tackle them.

Assess how you are doing in all of those areas. And shore up ones that are weak if you can. There are books and websites that cover every one of those spokes and can help you strengthen them.

REACH OUT

FRIENDS AND FAMILY

When you are an alcoholic, relationships with friends and family can be fraught with difficulty. It's called a 'family disease' for good reason.

But they are a critical part of your success.

Remember that the three best predictors of success in recovery are:

- Social support from family and friends

- Social standing-the things that give you esteem and dignity-like your job and your home

- Cognitive functioning-how well your brain continues to function

And data has shown that one-year recovery rates for alcoholics are 60 to 80% if you have both an intact family and intact job. With only one of those it drops to 30 to 40% after one year. If you were missing both, it drops in half again to 15 to 20%.[24]

When you don't have support from important people in your life, this can lead to setbacks. Interpersonal problems (relationship problems) are a large factor in relapse with data showing that negative emotional states and interpersonal problems serve as triggers for more than one-half of all relapses.[19]

All of this points to the importance of working on rebuilding or strengthening connections with the people that are important to you. (Or if it's too late for that, building new relationships with new supports).

As with other spokes on the wheel, there is a lot of available information on building and strengthening relationships available in books and online.

From the perspective of your medication journey, however, one of the most important things to keep in mind is that your family and friends can get the 'option myopia' problem we discussed earlier too.

They can be very focused and set on a particular solution for you, and unsupportive of all other solutions.

They can pin their hopes and dreams on you and on a particular solution working. And when you relapse they can feel despair and hopelessness, and this can lead to anger.

Remember, they are a product of this society—one which looks at alcoholism as a personality disorder—just as much as anyone may be.

Your family may need gentle help to open their eyes to other available solutions. And if they are on board with the solution you choose to pursue (whatever that may be), then it will be easier for you to gain their support and encouragement.

One major pitfall to watch out for is this: If you have tried to be abstinent, and then choose to try an 'as needed' approach that encourages drinking to be successful, then it is critical that you try to help your friends and family understand the approach first.

Otherwise you may find yourself with little support.

If picking up a bottle again will signal the end of your marriage and career, then an 'as needed' medication may not be the one to start with.

If you have decided to pursue medication then one thing which may help is to introduce them to the same materials that you have looked at. I hope that this book might be one of those materials. The top resources I would recommend showing them include:

- Book–The End of My Addiction by Dr. Olivier Ameisen[35] (Particularly if you decide to take baclofen).

- Documentary–One Little Pill by Adam Schomer and Claudia Christian, which is available to stream online.[39] (Particularly if you decide to take any 'as needed' medication, such as naltrexone or nalmefene).

- Article–The Irrationality of Alcoholics Anonymous, published in The Atlantic (theatlantic.com)[40]

- Forums–mywayout.org/community   and thesinclairmethod.net

- Additional resources specific to each medication are found in the FAQ sections of Book 4

SUPPORTS AROUND YOU

No matter what kind of illness you have, the greater the support you have for recovery, the more likely you will be to succeed.

Some individuals have been very successful with disulfiram, sometimes because they have had the assistance of a partner who watches them take it each and every day. This requires commitment and support.

Tolerating side-effects, tolerating drinking, the cost of medication, trying multiple medications before succeeding, and going through the hassle of a medical and recovery system that has not advanced as quickly as it should have in regards to addiction treatment is not easy for the alcoholic or your support network.

It's hard to watch someone we love struggle. But it's a little easier if they are going down a treatment path that we understand.

Assess the support you have around you in relation to the medication you choose. If you have support, engage those individuals early on in the best way you can.

ONLINE

There is a wealth of information and insight to be found in online forums about these drugs. I really cannot recommend these forums enough as an important part of your journey.

Most people in the medical community will advise that there is a lot of misinformation to be found in online forums, and this is very true.

But they also will provide you with insight and support that you may be able to find nowhere else.

In general (there are exceptions to every rule), here is what I have observed to be helpful and not-so-helpful about online forums:

Good for:

- Other's personal experiences—what worked and what didn't

- Immediate help for questions—for example, "Has anyone else experienced this side effect?"

- Encouragement and support from a group of people on the same path as you—an excellent reminder that you are not alone and that you are part of a community (can be helpful if you lack other supports)

- Clarification or translation of medical/research jargon and theory into actual experience and more easily understood language

- Troubleshooting when you run into barriers. For example, you can ask, "I can't get this medication from my pharmacist anymore—what should I do?'

- A place to help others and feel good about yourself

- Interaction and insights between alcoholics and family/friends of alcoholics (we need help to gain perspective on each other's' worlds and experiences)

I have learned to take with a grain of salt (or ignore altogether):

- Insights into very scientific specifics about why or how the medications work or the inner-workings of alcoholism within one's brain

- Information about areas that are extremely complicated or require in-depth scientific knowledge

- Some people may be very opinionated about and focused on their solution (option myopia) and less open-minded about other solutions

- People on forums suffer from the same stereotypes and stigma as people everywhere—even alcoholics spread stigma

- Negativity—there are sick people everywhere and 'hurt people   can   hurt   people'

03 | FOR CAREGIVERS

Courage to change the things I can,
and the wisdom to know the difference.

RETHINKING ENABLING

I think one of the saddest things about many illnesses—but particularly brain illnesses—is that it is sometimes difficult to ask for help—and then when we do, sometimes it feels like a door is shut in our face over and over again.

The hurdles and hoops people with alcoholism have to jump through to reach help sometimes is tragic.

How do you get to the clinic an hour away, on time for the appointment, when you have no money, no vehicle, can't stay sober, can't sleep, are dealing with marital problems, bankruptcy, legal issues?

How do you coherently and convincingly advocate for yourself that you'd like a referral or a prescription or housing assistance, or access to a fax machine or computer to send the referral to the next place, while your doctor (who has either become hardened to you due to your lies and drunken behavior; or doesn't know you from Adam) looks at you suspiciously and dismissively and asks you to go home and please shower.

Obtaining the medications in this book, and the right help is NOT an easy thing.

There are enormous barriers—how do you even find out about them unless you have strong cognitive ability and an appetite for seeking and reading medical research?

What if you don't have access to the internet? No health card? No credit card? No money?

Even if you convince your doctor to prescribe you one, will they prescribe the next one when that one doesn't work?

The one that could work for you may not even be available in your country. It might not be available at your pharmacy. It might not be available to you in your country through online ordering. It might be exorbitantly priced.

What a headache.

Imagine if we made cancer sufferers go through so much to obtain treatment?

It amazes me that anyone ever gets help.

As caregivers (friends or family of an alcoholic), I know that some of the 'principles' taught to those of us who have addicts in our lives are:

- Don't be an 'enabler'
- They have to want to get (and then go and get) help themselves
- Don't cause a crisis, but don't stand in the way of one either
- They have to hit rock bottom–don't cushion their fall

These principles imply a very 'hands off' approach.

But when it comes to getting and accessing help (and maybe having to get and access many different solutions before one of them does help), I think addicts need all the help, support and enabling behavior they can possibly get.

THE FAMILY DISEASE

If you are the friend or family member of an alcoholic, then you have most likely been affected by the family disease of alcoholism.

An enormous burden is placed on friends and family members of those who suffer from alcoholism.

Obtaining and taking medication (and finding the right medication) can be a straightforward process.

But more often it's not.

You don't have to *lead* this process of getting your alcoholic on medication, but it's important to know that your involvement–your support, love, time, help and encouragement–may be the difference between life or death for your alcoholic. My friend Randy is dead because he didn't get the support and help he needed in time.

Information is power. I encourage you to read this book and do your own research.

And get the right support. You will *not* get support for a medical approach from the vast majority of 12-step program family groups or treatment centers. As the Alanon adage goes–don't go to the hardware store for milk. And don't go to a 12-step program for support for a medical approach.

Look instead to medication-related online support groups where family and friends of other alcoholics that are taking medication help each other. There you'll get the right encouragement and support.

RELAPSE HAPPENS

Relapse is a part of the disease of alcoholism. If your loved one never relapses, they probably were never an alcoholic to begin with.

As family and friends, how do we deal with this?

Here is the truth: Your alcoholic's relapse is not a personal affront to you. It has nothing to do with you. It is not a reflection on whether they love you enough or not. Get over that.

If your alcoholic is dependent enough on alcohol, they may have little to no control left over relapse. Alcoholism is a disease where circuits in the brain necessary for free will are eroded.

React the way you would react if anyone you loved relapsed with any other another disease. It's not personal. QTIP – Quit Taking it Personally.

04 | DRUG BY DRUG DETAIL

*"There is no other field in psychiatric research that has,
in recent years, yielded so many novel, druggable targets
and innovative treatment strategies than for alcohol
addiction."*[8]

–Dr. Rainer Spanagel, Director of the Institute of
Psychopharmacology, University of Heidelberg

THE DRUG LISTS

Drug Groupings

I've divided up the medications covered in this book (and in much greater detail in Book 4) into several groups. These groupings are somewhat arbitrary because there is no clear way to really rank or rate medications.

As mentioned earlier, sometimes medications are referred to by the medical community as 'first line', 'second line', etc., depending upon whether a medication is a 'go to' medication for a condition, or a secondary medication to try if the first one fails or is not appropriate.

I have avoided using these terms since they can be misleading.

While I might try to start with one or more of the medications on the A-List myself, there are so many factors to take into consideration (discussed in the previous chapter), that you may find something on the B-List or even on the Futures List which might just be a very good fit for you.

The groupings I've created include:

1) The A-List: Most Important Medications for Today

2) The B-List: Medications Worth Consideration Today

3) The D-List: Eleven Drugs that May *Increase* Drinking

4) The Futures List: Sixty+ Drugs to Watch

Please note–don't confuse alcoholism 'Types' with the naming of these lists. They are not related at all.

Both Type A and Type B alcoholics may find medications that work for them on either the A-List or B-List.

THE A-LIST: MOST IMPORTANT MEDICATIONS FOR TODAY

The 'Most Important' medications are those which either have a lot of research and leading researchers backing them; are FDA-approved either for other medical conditions or for the treatment of alcohol dependence; and/or have a lot of promise for some other reason or a combination of reasons for their use against alcohol dependence.

My focus in putting together this list is the evidence of efficacy (effectiveness).

This does not necessarily mean that they will be the easiest to attain.

These are generally the medications most commonly tried by those who are investigating and taking medications for treatment of alcoholism for the first time, and they may also have significant anecdotal support for their effectiveness.

These medications include:

- Acamprosate

- Baclofen (High Dose)

- Topiramate

- Naltrexone (Daily Dosage, As Needed or by Injection)

- Nalmefene

- Gabapentin & Pregabalin

THE B-LIST: MEDICATIONS WORTH CONSIDERATION TODAY

The medications I have classified as 'Worth Consideration Today' have less supporting evidence (possibly due to a lack of research, not necessarily due to lack of potential), or may not seem to be quite as effective or appropriate for as many individuals.

Most of them still have a fair amount of top-level research or pharmaceutical support based on trial evidence.

With further research and greater understanding of how they work, any of these might join the A-List (or drop further down the list).

All of the medications on this list are FDA-Approved, but only one is FDA-Approved for the treatment of alcoholism.

These medications include:

- Ondansetron

- Varenicline

- Disulfiram

- Prazosin & Doxazosin

- Zonisamide

- Olanzapine

- Sertraline

- Sodium Oxybate (SO) (See caveats around this one in the section specifically focusing on SO)

THE D-LIST: USE CAUTION

The D-List contains medications that, in at least one study (in either lab animals or humans), have been shown to *increase* drinking.

These medications include:

- Sertraline

- Doxazosin

- Ondansetron

- Atomoxetine

- Fluoxetine & Venlafaxine

- Flupenthixol Decanoate, Amisulpride, Tiapride

- Lisuride

- Ritanserin

- Tiagabine

THE FUTURES-LIST: SIXTY+ MEDICATIONS TO WATCH

Medications I have classified as 'To Watch' have either recently been researched for alcohol dependence with promising results or findings or have some other indication (such as filing of patents) that indicate they may be worth watching.

These medications could ultimately be proven ineffective or in some way dangerous, or with more research and discovery they could eventually top the A-list.

It's worth noting that at the time that Amiesen started experimenting with baclofen for example (which I've placed on the A-List), it would have also fallen into the B- or Futures List due to the very limited, but somewhat promising research on it.

There are approximately 60 different medications on this list, which are listed and covered in Book 4 of this book series.

05 | RESOURCES

APRESCRIPTIONFORALCOHOLICS.C OM

If you would like additional information on this topic, I encourage you to visit the book website, located at APrescriptionForAlcoholics.com.

There you will find:

- At least one free book excerpt that you can share with others.

- A list of recommended reading which includes some of the best and most informative research articles, reports, popular press articles, and books.

You'll also find links to:

- Key research, reports, and publications mentioned in this book

- Forums and support groups

- Links to online pharmacies

The site will be updated and expanded over time, so please join the mailing list for updates.

SPREAD THE WORD

If this book or the medications in it have made a difference to you, please consider helping to spread the word.

You can do this by:

- Sharing the free chapter found on the website with a friend (www.APrescriptionforAlcoholics.com)

- Passing the book on to someone you know.

- Donating a few copies to a library, school, doctor's office or recovery program.

- Posting about the book on social media.

BIBLIOGRAPHY

1. Heilig M, Egli M. Pharmacological treatment of alcohol dependence: Target symptoms and target mechanisms. *Pharmacol Ther.* 2006;111(3):855-876. doi:10.1016/j.pharmthera.2006.02.001.

2. Batki SL, Pennington DL. Toward personalized medicine in the pharmacotherapy of alcohol use disorder: Targeting patient genes and patient goals. *Am J Psychiatry.* 2014;171(4):391-394. doi:10.1176/appi.ajp.2014.14010061.

3. Addiction Medicine: Closing the Gap Between Science & Practice | CASAColumbia. http://www.casacolumbia.org/addiction-research/reports/addiction-medicine. Accessed November 11, 2015.

4. Heilig M. The Thirteenth Step Addiction in the Age of Brain Science. 2015.

5. Ferri M, Amato L, Davoli M. Alcoholics Anonymous and other 12-step programmes for alcohol dependence. *Cochrane Database Syst Rev.* 2006;3(3):CD005032. doi:10.1002/14651858.CD005032.pub2.

6. White N. Alcoholics Anonymous has a terrible success rate, addiction expert finds. *Tor Star.* 2014:2-5. http://www.thestar.com/life/2014/03/28/alcoholics_anonymous_has_a_terrible_success_rate_addiction_expert_finds.html.

7. Author Unknown. Medication for the Treatment of Alcohol Use Disorder: A Brief Guide. *NIAAA.* 2013. http://store.samhsa.gov/shin/content/SMA15-4907/SMA15-4907.pdf.

8. Spanagel R, Vengeliene V. New pharmacological treatment strategies for relapse prevention. *Curr Top Behav Neurosci.* 2013;13:583-609. doi:10.1007/7854_2012_205.

9. Volkow ND, Fowler JS, Wang GJ, Baler R, Telang F. Imaging dopamine's role in drug abuse and addiction.

Neuropharmacology. 2009;56 Suppl 1:3-8. doi:10.1016/j.neuropharm.2008.05.022.

10. In Clue to Addiction, Brain Injury Halts Smoking - New York Times. http://www.nytimes.com/2007/01/26/science/26brain.ht ml?_r=0. Accessed May 26, 2015.

11. Naqvi NH, Bechara A. The hidden island of addiction: the insula. *Trends Neurosci.* 2009;32(1):56-67. doi:10.1016/j.tins.2008.09.009.

12. Video & Transcript: President Obama Speech in Charleston, West Virginia on Prescription Drug Abuse and Heroin Addiction, Oct. 21, 2015 | Shallow Nation. http://www.shallownation.com/2015/10/21/video-president-obama-speech-in-charleston-west-virginia-on-prescription-drug-abuse-and-heroin-addiction-oct-21-2015/. Accessed October 29, 2015.

13. Dealing With Addiction: Why The 20th Century Was Wrong: Peter Ferentzy: 9781105004100: Amazon.com: Books. http://www.amazon.com/Dealing-With-Addiction-Century-Wrong/dp/1105004104. Accessed October 27, 2015.

14. Clinical relevance of alcohol reduction | Progress in Mind: Focus on Alcohol Use Disorders Resource Centre. http://progressinmind.elsevierresource.com/videos/lectures/clinical-relevance-alcohol-reduction. Accessed October 5, 2015.

15. Lewandowski CM. SAMHSA - Reasons for Not Receiving Treatment. 2014;1. doi:10.1017/CBO9781107415324.004.

16. Unknown. Lundbeck Shareholder Magazine. 2011.

17. Rehm J. The risks associated with alcohol use and alcoholism. *Alcohol Res Health.* 2011;34(2):135-143. doi:Fea-AR&H-65.

18. L B. [Benefits in reducing alcohol consumption□: how nalmefene can help]. PubMed Commons. *Encephale.* 2015;40(6):2014-2015. doi:10.1016/j.encep.2014.10.012.

19. Larimer ME, Palmer RS, Marlatt GA. Relapse prevention: An overview of Marlatt's Cognitive-Cehavioral Model. *Alcohol Res Heal.* 1999;23(2):151-160. doi:10.1186/1747-597X-6-17.

20. Sinclair J, Chick J, Sørensen P, Kiefer F, Batel P, Gual A.

Can Alcohol Dependent Patients Adhere to an "As-Needed" Medication Regimen? *Eur Addict Res.* 2014;20(5):209-217. doi:10.1159/000357865.

21. What Addicts Need. http://www.newsweek.com/what-addicts-need-93767. Accessed October 23, 2015.

22. Leavitt SB. Evidence for the Efficacy of Naltrexone in the Treatment of Alcohol Dependence (Alcoholism). *Addict Treat Forum.* 2002.

23. Soyka M, Rösner S. Opioid antagonists for pharmacological treatment of alcohol dependence - a critical review. *Curr Drug Abuse Rev.* 2008;1(3):280-291.

24. Inside Addiction Treatment With Dr. Marvin Seppala | The Fix. https://www.thefix.com/content/inside-addiction-with-marvin-seppala. Accessed October 30, 2015.

25. Weerts E, Kaminski BJ. Comparison of baclofen vs. naltrexone treatment during abstinence on reinstatement of alcohol self-administration in baboons. *Drug Alcohol Depend.* 2015;146:e18-e19. doi:10.1016/j.drugalcdep.2014.09.731.

26. Porjesz B, Rangaswamy M, Kamarajan C, Jones K a., Padmanabhapillai A, Begleiter H. The utility of neurophysiological markers in the study of alcoholism. *Clin Neurophysiol.* 2005;116(5):993-1018. doi:10.1016/j.clinph.2004.12.016.

27. Johnson B a. Medication treatment of different types of alcoholism. *Am J Psychiatry.* 2010;167(6):630-639. doi:10.1176/appi.ajp.2010.08101500.

28. Kranzler HR, Armeli S, Tennen H, et al. A double-blind, randomized trial of sertraline for alcohol dependence: moderation by age and 5-hydroxytryptamine transporter-linked promoter region genotype. *J Clin Psychopharmacol.* 2011;31(1):22-30. doi:10.1016/j.ypsy.2011.07.076.

29. Johnson B a., Seneviratne C, Wang XQ, Daoud NA, Li MD. Determination of genotype combinations that can predict the outcome of the treatment of alcohol dependence using the 5-HT3 antagonist ondansetron. *Am J Psychiatry.* 2013;170(9):1020-1031. doi:10.1176/appi.ajp.2013.12091163.

30. Neergaard L. In a lab that looks like a bar, researchers hunt new ways to curb heavy drinking. *Chicago Trib.* 2015:2-4. http://www.chicagotribune.com/lifestyles/health/sns-bc-

us-med--healthbeat-alcohol-treatment-20150101-story.html.

31.   Dundon W, Lynch KG, Pettinati HM, Lipkin C, Alcohol B. Dependence 6 Months After Serotonergic. *Alcohol.* 2006;28(7):1065-1073. http://www.pubmedcentral.nih.gov/articlerender.fcgi?artid =1435448&tool=pmcentrez&rendertype=abstract. Accessed June 15, 2015.

32.   Haass-Koffler CL, Leggio L, Kenna G a. Pharmacological Approaches to Reducing Craving in Patients with Alcohol Use Disorders. *CNS Drugs.* 2014;28(4):1-18. doi:10.1007/s40263-014-0149-3.

33.   Kenna GA, Haass-Koffler CL, Zywiak WH, et al. Role of the α1 blocker doxazosin in alcoholism: a proof-of-concept randomized controlled trial. *Addict Biol.* 2015. doi:10.1111/adb.12275.

34.   Lunau K. Off-label drugs are off the charts in Canada - Macleans.ca. *Macleans Mag.* 2012. http://www.macleans.ca/society/health/off-label-is-off-the-charts/. Accessed June 16, 2015.

35.   Ameisen O. The End of My Addiction. 2008. http://us.macmillan.com/theendofmyaddiction/olivieramei sen. Accessed May 18, 2015.

36.   Miller K. Off-Label Drug Use : What You Need to Know Prescription drugs are often prescribed for uses other than what the. *WebMD.* 2015.

37.   Kelvin Ogilvie AE. Prescription Pharmaceuticals in Canada - Off-Label Use. *Standing Senat Comm Soc Aff.* 2014.

38.   Lee MR, Leggio L. Combined Pharmacotherapies for the Management of Alcoholism: Rationale and Evidence to Date. *CNS Drugs.* 2014;28(2):107-119. doi:10.1007/s40263-013-0137-z.

39.   Christian C. One Little Pill Documentary about Naltrexone and TSM. *Vimeo.com.* 2014. https://vimeo.com/ondemand/onelittlepill.

40.   Glaser G. The Irrationality of Alcoholics Anonymous. *Atl.* 2015. http://www.theatlantic.com/features/archive/2015/03/the -irrationality-of-alcoholics-anonymous/386255/. Accessed April 28, 2015.

Printed in Great Britain
by Amazon

82879192R00071